Good Practice Guide: **Fee Management**

RIBA Good Practice Guides

Other titles in this series:

Building Condition Surveys, by Mike Hoxley

Employment, by Brian Gegg and David Sharp

Extensions of Time, by Gillian Birkby, Albert Ponte and Frances Alderson

Inspecting Works, by Nicholas Jamieson

Keeping Out of Trouble, by Owen Luder

Marketing your Practice, edited by Helen Elias

Mediation, by Andy Grossman

Negotiating the Planning Maze, by John Collins and Philip Moren

Painless Financial Management, by Brian Pinder-Ayres

Starting a Practice, by Simon Foxell

Good Practice Guide:
Fee Management

Roland Phillips

RIBA Publishing

© Roland Phillips, 2009
Published by RIBA Publishing, 15 Bonhill Street, London EC2P 2EA

ISBN 978 1 85946 180 8

Stock Code 61859

The right of Roland Phillips to be identified as the Author of this Work have been asserted in accordance with the Copyright, Designs and Patents Act 1988 Sections 77 and 78.

British Library Cataloguing-in-Publication Data
A catalogue record for this book is available from the British Library.

Publisher: Steven Cross
Commissioning Editor: James Thompson
Project Editor: Alasdair Deas
Editor: Andrea Platts
Designed by Ben Millbank
Typeset by Academic + Technical
Printed and bound by MPG Books, Cornwall

While every effort has been made to ensure the accuracy and quality of information in this publication, the Publisher accepts no responsibility for the subsequent use of this information, for any errors or omissions that it may contain, or for any misunderstandings arising from it.

RIBA Publishing is part of RIBA Enterprises Ltd.
www.ribaenterprises.com

Series foreword

The *RIBA Good Practice Guide* series has been specifically developed to provide architects, and other construction professionals, with practical advice and guidance on a range of topics that affect them, and the management of their business, on a day-to-day basis.

All of the guides in the series are written in an easy-to-read, straightforward style. The guides are not meant to be definitive texts on the particular subject in question, but each guide will be the reader's first point of reference, offering them a quick overview of the key points and then providing them with a 'route map' for finding further, more detailed information. Where appropriate, checklists, tables, diagrams and case studies will be included to aid ease of use.

Good Practice Guide: Fee Management

It is said that architectural services are worth only as much as the client is willing to pay, regardless of what they cost to provide. This may be so, but it is also clear that the value the practice itself puts on its work – and the way in which it communicates that to the client – also influences their worth. As Roland Phillips points out in this excellent book, the client's opinion of the architect will be coloured by the transparency and fairness of the fee offer and the way in which that fee is amended through the course of the project. Quite rightly, all clients are after 'value for money' – it is down to the architect to persuade them that this is not the same as 'cheap', that value and cost are not the same.

This point is critical. Over the past few decades (and especially with the OFT's ban on our publishing recommended fee scales), the scrabble for work in the design-and-build world order has lured us to undervalue our services to the extent that we are at or near the bottom of professional fee-earning league. The work that architects do requires special capabilities and can deliver not only fine and functional design but a built heritage to grace our communities for many years. Good architecture improves people's lives and adds value. Its production deserves to be properly compensated.

How much to charge for architectural services is a delicate question of fundamental importance that, self-evidently, goes to the heart of the business success of all practices. More than that, fee levels are a reflection of the value and status that the wider community bestows on our profession as a whole.

As this guide shows, to get the fee right the practice must know what its services will cost and understand the business risks for both the client and the project. The whole process is carefully dissected here: assessing risks, the methods of calculating fees, successfully negotiating the fee, getting paid, managing change, and much more. The underlying philosophy is sympathetic to the problems and pressures that we and our clients face, and I recommend it to you unreservedly.

Ruth Reed
President, RIBA

About the author

Roland Phillips RIBA commenced his professional life with Tecton in 1948; subsequently becoming a partner in private practice, until joining the National Health Service, practising as a regional architect and finally as managing director of the project management division of a plc.

He has served on the RIBA Contracts Committee, the RIBA Appointments Group, the Joint Contracts Tribunal and is editor of RIBA Agreements.

Acknowledgements

I acknowledge the wisdom of the many authors of reports on this important subject in *RIBA Journal* Practice pages, contributors to RIBAnet, authors quoted in the text and their publishers and, in particular, I acknowledge the permission to quote or paraphrase the guidance given by Michael Brown, Robert Campbell, Steven Lockley, Owen Luder, Sarah Lupton, M. Paul Nicholson, Brian Pinder-Ayres and Steven Yakeley.

I am also grateful to Jane Duncan RIBA, Vice President Practice, Richard Brindley, RIBA Executive Director of Professional Services, Adrian Dobson, RIBA Director of Practice, and Francis Phillips and to Matthew Thompson, Anna Walters and Alasdair Deas at RIBA Publishing.

Roland Phillips RIBA

October 2009

Contents

Introduction

As Owen Luder has said: 'Cash is king! If you run out of money – you go bust'.

This is particularly pertinent at this time in the midst of a financial recession – 'the credit crunch' – when getting paid will be a particular priority for architects.

The aim of this guide is to encourage the development of sound and effective systems in fee management for any project or any role and for managing time, cost and payments.

However, the client's attitudes will impact on the architect's costs also. Average fees – as in recommended fee scales, now outlawed by competition law – are unlikely to reflect the real cost of a specific project or the resources required.

There is no 'quick-fix' method for establishing the right fee for a particular job. Getting the fee right and getting paid for all the work done can only be achieved if the practice knows what its services will cost and understands the business risks of the client and the project.

"There is no 'quick-fix' method for establishing the right fee for a particular job"

Equally important factors are the value the practice puts on its own work and the client's perception of the added value of the architect's services.

But added value is not a constant, each project will generate its own benefits – these may be cash returns for a developer, or better or improved facilities for a business, hospital or school. Other projects may arise just out of necessity.

Some clients may not want 'art', only effective delivery. Others know the advantage of having both. Some clients drive Rolls Royce cars, others, second-hand Fiestas.

The subject cannot be covered on one side of A4 paper, but the 'golden rules for a healthy fee regime' laid out in Section 7 of this guide encapsulate many of the important issues:

- Always have a comprehensive agreement in writing.
- Make certain that the client understands the payment provisions.
- Use RIBA Agreements, wherever possible.
- Don't start any significant work until the agreement is signed.
- Carefully evaluate the cost of providing the services.
- Get the client to sign off and pay for:
  - the relevant work before initiating any activities with third parties, such as making applications to statutory or local authorities for planning or building regulations, or to freeholders or inviting tenders, and
  - each work stage as completed.
- Establish rigorous procedures for managing fee accounts, including routine credit-checking of clients.
- Keep a separate fee file, with copies of the agreement, all fee correspondence, file notes and submitted fee accounts. Keep it up to date at all times.
- Invoice monthly on every commission for any amount due, no matter how small.
- Submit claims for additional fees as incurred, not at the end of the commission – claiming additional fees on completion of the commission can surprise the client and lead to argument, late payment or, even worse, a counterclaim for some alleged negligence.

Examples given in this guide are related to the architect's traditional role for a simple building project, but the principles behind the examples are transferable to any role or service that the architect is to perform; including, for instance, as project manager or as technical due diligence auditor in a PPP or PFI project.

Section 1
Fees and the business of architecture

In this Section:

- *Good design really pays!*
- *The business of architecture*
- *Valuing your work*
- *Bringing the product to the market-place*
- *Putting a realistic price on the product*
- *Making a profit*
- *Establishing robust management procedures*
- *Fee management*
- *Regular monitoring of performance*

> *The profession must ensure that it associates design with added value of all kinds; learns to value itself more and agree a fee basis, or other means of financial return, appropriate to such valuable intellectual property.*
>
> Marco Goldschmied, President RIBA, 'Meeting the Challenge –
> A strategy for architecture and architects 1999–2003', *RIBA Journal*,
> November 1999

Good design really pays!

It is a common mantra that 'Good design really pays', but 'How much?' and 'To whom?'

It has been said that quality is what the customer wants, but only high quality will bring delight. To achieve that result the product must meet the customer's aspirations within cost and time parameters and, in the case of a building project, the client must receive complete and integrated information.

Clients that benefit from good design generally receive the benefit as a result of value assessments made during the design process, whether those assessments are made using explicit value management (VM) techniques or by the iterative nature of the design process. Formal VM techniques are used to assess the value of design solutions or decisions, examining the balance between initial costs and life-time costs.

Wouldn't it be brilliant if similar assessments were made of the designer's fees, which can be so significant but are only a small part of the overall cost? Until that glorious day, the message is clear; if architects are to achieve adequate rewards, they must offer quality of service, excellence of design and rigorous business systems.

> *In my view, the architect's fee can be the best value item of a whole building project. But then I'm the sort of person who thinks that the chef is the most important person in the restaurant. Not that the waiters and the maitre d' aren't important of course, but however good the decor or the service, if the food isn't any good – what's the point?*
>
> Gus Alexander, *Building*, 20 April 2001

The business of architecture

Many commentators have noted that architects have the commitment and determination required for entrepreneurial success, but do not display the skills to manage themselves efficiently.

> *The profession itself should treat architecture as a profession and as a business, not just an exciting and a liberating profession.*
>
> M. Paul Nicholson

> *It's a tough world and if you can't deal with the battle front – that's the administrative, legal and financial stuff – then you shouldn't be an architect.*
>
> Sir Nicolas Grimshaw, *RIBA Journal*, February 2005

The objectives of any commercial venture, whatever its size, include:

- understanding the market and its risks
- putting a realistic price on the product and bringing it to the market-place
- making a profit

and require

- the establishment of robust management procedures

- regular monitoring of professional performance
- regular monitoring of financial performance.

In this section these objectives are examined briefly in the context of the 'price of the product', i.e. the fee. Fees may be the life-blood of the practice, but robust business practices are a prerequisite. The wider aspects of running a practice are covered in *The Architect's Handbook of Practice Management,* 7th edition, referred to in this book as '*The Handbook*', and in RIBA Good Practice Guides, in particular *Painless Financial Management*.

In the *Architects' Journal* (2 February 2006) Adam Bernstein identified a number of programmes which can help with business needs of architectural businesses, large or small, including:

- www.businesslink.gov.uk – providing advice on health and safety, IT and e-commerce, employment, taxation, finance and marketing
- www.shellstep.org.uk – to assist in harnessing the skills of undergraduates to undertake subsidised, predefined business-related projects
- www.bre.co.uk/clip – for developing best practice and increasing productivity as part of the Construction Lean Improvement Programme
- www.constructionline.co.uk – who assess consultants for prequalification for public sector organisations.

> When it comes to improving profits and cash flow the golden rule is: what you can measure, you can manage. The better you monitor your cash flow the better you can improve it. Some improvements can be made from adopting a more businesslike attitude towards billing and debt collection, others from making the best of the tax system.
>
> Andrew Rhodes of Sobell Rhodes Chartered Accountants,
> *RIBA Journal,* July 2004

Valuing your work

Architects' fees have become an emotive as well as a practical issue since the EU and the Office of Fair Trading decided that recommended fees were anti-competitive, compounded by the decline in the influence of architects (or society's interest in architectural values) and competition from other disciplines.

There is no entitlement to any particular level of fees. Deciding on the fee is therefore a potentially complex task. In addition to costs and profit, the fee

"There is no entitlement to any particular level of fees"

has to cover perceived risks. Risks are particularly difficult to assess, and, in any case, the outcomes are dependent on the degree of good or bad luck.

Inevitably, at the end of the commission the client's opinion of the architect will be influenced by the simplicity or transparency and fairness of the fee. Even the most opulent clients will expect 'value for money' in accordance with their own perception. The fee offer is therefore critical to reputation as well as to the financial well-being of the practice.

Understanding the practice's strengths and weaknesses in this area is vital for success and peace of mind. Consider the following questions:

- Who are the target clients?
- What is the position of the practice in that market?
- Who are the likely competitors? If they always undercut a rational fee, is the practice in the right market?
- In many cases the fee is just another cost to the client. Is the practice worth it? Or more? Does the practice have a reputation for added value beyond the client's original expectation?

> *The tradition of the architect as the 'struggling artist' is still evident – particularly amongst the profession's many sole practitioners – creating tension with the role of architectural practices as businesses creating value meeting their stakeholders' needs. Architects are viewed as risk-averse, unwilling to take responsibility and therefore the risk and reward for their work.*
> RIBA Constructive Change: an industry study, September 2005

Bringing the product to the market-place

A marketing strategy is essential for every practice. A practice statement, whether a brochure or a website, should be available for any enquirer or included in the annual RIBA *Directory of Practices*, which is sent to some 5,000 potential clients, or in the regional directories published by some RIBA Regions.

It goes without saying that completed projects are the best tools for marketing the practice. Clients, contractors, other consultants, the bank manager can all be encouraged to spread the word about the practice's reputation, provided, of course, that it is good!

Other methods will include meeting potential clients by joining the local Chamber of Commerce or the Federation of Small Businesses, or going to Confederation of British Industry or the Institute of Directors networking events.

Could the practice's position be improved by joining a small practice network? Regional offices of the RIBA may be able to help in making contact with local networks. *Small Practice Networks,* a RIBA Booklet (June 1999, ISBN 1 85946 062 3) provides useful guidance.

In particular, a network may be another source of information when calculating a fee proposal or perhaps for creating a joint venture to bid for larger projects.

> *During the last turndown in the economy the local architects in the town got together and ran a six-session evening course on the process of renovating your house. For one of the sessions we even had the building inspector present. On the last evening we had 'speed dating an architect', where you could speak to three different architects for 20 minutes to see how they would resolve the problem. The course was well attended, the presenters and all the local architects who did the speed dating were paid for teaching the course, and we got work out of it. And the local architects networked with each other, which has paid off for years to come as we now view ourselves as part of a 'family' and look after each other.*
>
> RIBAnet, 19 July 2006

Putting a realistic price on the product

> *The only element of a professional service that can be measured is the time taken to provide it. All the hours in the working day have a price; there is no 'free' time – salaries have to be paid and the costs of running the business have to be met.*
>
> *The Handbook*

The crucial management tool in job costing is the time sheet, which records the time spent on project work, marketing, management and administration and absences. The question then arises of how the cost of non-project time is to be recovered.

See also: Appendix C, page 95

The ratio of chargeable to non-chargeable time should be kept under review. If this ratio can be improved, profitability should also improve. See also the 2007/08 Business Benchmarking Report prepared for the RIBA (page 34).

Making a profit (from *The Handbook*)

Profitability is not simply a matter of 'doing well' in the long term or achieving an increase in turnover; it should be seen as a quantifiable target for the performance of the business overall, as a target for each job in its own right and for each fee-earning person employed by the practice.

In times of high inflation, a practice that is breaking even on paper is, in real terms, operating at a loss. It follows that setting a level of overall profitability that relates realistically to an uneconomic climate can be a matter of survival. In more stable market conditions, profitability is something that a practice might feel able to take a view about, in line with its character and philosophy.

"Profits can be eaten away by sloppy commissioning procedures"

Profits can be eaten away by sloppy commissioning procedures. The income expected from each project should be established in the terms of the commission agreed with the client and described in a properly formulated written agreement. If the client subsequently asks for additional services, the client must pay for them. The commission must not be allowed to 'creep' into something more than what was defined in the agreement. Profits are also dissipated by underestimating the time needed to complete a job and by allocating too much, or inappropriate staff effort to it.

Establishing robust management procedures

Setting realistic profit margins depends on a precise knowledge of costs – the cost of running the practice overall, the cost of running each job and the chargeable and actual cost of each of the people employed by the practice.

The price of time will vary with:

• the quality or value of the services required, and
• the competence of the people necessary to deliver the services.

The varied and fluctuating nature of commissions does not permit architects to set a once-for-all pattern of costing that will assure profitability. Even if the arithmetic is sound, there is always the variability of human factors – key staff may leave or fall ill, there may be a disagreement on policy between partners, or a misunderstanding may arise with the client.

Watchful and responsible management and risk assessment procedures, supported and implemented by sound technical and financial procedures, will always be needed.

Managing the workload of the office is also a key factor. Ensuring that work gets done on time and knowing whether or not the resources are available to take on new offers of work means planning who will be doing what and when, and then monitoring what happens in reality.

To achieve this, it is important to have an integrated methodology for the supporting business processes by appointing one person to have overall responsibility for the task.

The practice management toolbox (outlined in Appendix A) will need to include systems for:

- recording time usage and calculating the cost of that time
- day-to-day accounting or book-keeping
- resource planning
- resource monitoring
- calculating fee offers
- invoicing clients, and
- identifying the practice's workload over time and monitoring progress.

Each system should provide the information required by the others. The data may be collected manually or electronically, in commercially available systems or those developed in-house. Commercial software packages can provide each system separately or in combination in compatible formats to allow easy integration of the data, particularly with an accounting package. Some systems are available which also manage documents, e-mails, meetings, etc. as well as time, resources, costs and billing.

Fee management

The first and most important management rule is to have a signed agreement in place before undertaking any significant services.

See also: Section 6, Negotiating the fee, page 53 If negotiations with the client over the terms of appointment are protracted, but the client requires the work to start, ensure that a holding letter is sent to establish a debt. Procedures must be in place to monitor non-completion of the agreement at regular intervals.

- *Picardi v. Cuniberti* [2002] EWHC 2923 [QB]
- *Munkenbeck and Marshall v. Michael Harold* [2005] EWHC 356 [TCC]

These law cases arose where clients were sued for unpaid fees, but the plaintiffs lost because the agreements were not signed by the client and, in one case, the Conditions were only referred to but not given to the client. Although in each case the client was a domestic client and there were arguments about adjudicators' decisions, the important factor was non-completion of the agreement.

In another case, *Cartwright v. Fay*, where the adjudicator sued for unpaid fees, the court held that the client had agreed to the dispute resolution procedures by signing the building contract.

If you have a growing file of letters and notes of meetings relating to fee negotiations after you have started work on the project, beware: you are drifting into a 'moving goalposts' situation.

> *You will have difficulty enforcing a contract that has not been finalised, for until there is an unqualified offer and acceptance there is almost certainly no enforceable contract.*
>
> Owen Luder

Regular monitoring of performance

> *I would never say that cash flow is king, but I remain convinced that if you don't control it, it will certainly, probably for the worse, control you.*
> Christopher Ash of Project Orange, *RIBA Journal*, August 2006

Part of the practice's procedures will (or should) include regular review of individual projects and of financial performance of the practice. Efficient performance will benefit all those connected with the project – the client, the contractor, the designers and the practice's bank. Process is not the enemy of creativity. It is the lubricant.

"Process is not the enemy of creativity. It is the lubricant"

The *RIBA Good Practice Guide: Painless Financial Management* describes the several elements necessary for an effective accountancy regime and the *RIBA Outline Plan of Work 2007* (amended November 2008) provides a flexible framework for the process of managing and designing building projects and administering building contracts (see Section 3).

Project performance can be significantly improved by establishing appropriate procedures for work stage planning, monitoring progress, reports, handover and reviewing project performance (feedback), the objective of which is to examine performance by comparison with original targets and to extract or deduce useful information, which can be fed back to increase efficiency in the delivery of future projects.

See also: Appendix B, page 93

Of course, a review may be commissioned by the client for a long-term evaluation of the project (RIBA Work Stage L3), which will also provide useful insights into the architect's contributions. Customer satisfaction surveys, often also called 'feedback', will be part of any quality management system. A useful paper on this subject by Kim Birchall and Helen Elias was published in *RIBA Journal* in December 2005.

> *In its purest form the design process is a classic 'right-brain' activity. . . . The detailed recording of time is one of those left-brain activities that does not come readily to many architects.*
> *Good Practice Guide: Painless Financial Management*

Monitoring financial performance is not a creative activity (nor is it intended to be), but the routine book-keeping function can be tailored to show turnover, invoices sent and paid, bad debts, VAT, income tax and National Insurance payments and provisional profit and loss accounts and can identify critical elements to be kept under review or which demand instant action.

Income will be required to cover the costs of professional and technical salaries; administration costs; principals' drawings and profit or Company Directors' salaries and dividends; general office overheads; marketing; professional indemnity insurance; information technology; CPD; research and quality systems, etc.

Section 2
Benefits and risks of a fee offer

In this Section:

- *The invitation*
- *Benefits*
- *Risks*
- *The client*
- *Defining the commission*

The invitation

A client may invite an architect to make an offer:

- in one-to-one negotiation, on the basis of personal contact or recommendation, perhaps after an initial interview; this method is particularly suitable where the services required or the brief have not been finalised, or
- in competition with other architects. There are many tried and tested competitive processes which enable a client to select either an architect or a design solution:
  - *Competitive Interview* to find the right architect – expressions of interest are requested from registered architects, with a shortlist being selected for interview. Only a broad project brief is required, and a commitment to build.
  - *Open Ideas Competition* – this is run to identify a range of possible design solutions, against a broad conceptual brief, with no commitment to build.
  - *Open Project Competition* to find a single design solution – often a two-stage competition, open to all registered architects, with a detailed project brief and a commitment to build.
  - *Invited Competition* to find a single design solution – restricted to selected architects, with a detailed project brief and a commitment to build.

 – *Tailor-made Competitions* – the beauty of the competitive process is that it is completely flexible and can be adapted to meet the specific requirements of each client, and each project. Many clients choose to combine the design competition with the competitive interview.

Public contracts

Contracts for professional services may also be subject to the Public Contracts Regulations 2006 (SI 2006 No. 5). Regulation 3 defines a 'contracting authority', Regulation 30 sets out the criteria for awarding a contract and Regulation 30 is concerned with design contests. The regulations only apply to services which are likely to be above a certain threshold, which at the time of writing is €211,000.

The equivalent sterling threshold is £139,893 and does not follow currency fluctuations. The threshold will not be revised until 2010.

Responding to the client

Whatever the selection process, any approach from a potential client should be acknowledged at once. An action plan should be devised to analyse the benefits and risks to the practice if the commission is won, and if a team bid is required, procedures and terms with other professionals should be established.

If possible, establish that, when a bid in competition is required, the selection process will be fair to all competitors and will protect the copyright in any submitted material.

When an offer cannot be made against clear contractual obligations, for instance where the available information is insufficient to make a realistic assessment of the necessary resources, either:

See also:
Specimen
letter, page 16

- make a preliminary offer, perhaps for time-based charges, to carry out feasibility studies in order to define the scope of the project and the services required, or
- decline the invitation.

Benefits

The benefits to the practice of winning the commission may include:

- increased profit

- business expansion
- employment for the existing staff, perhaps avoiding redundancy.

Risks

'Risk' equals 'uncertainty'. To start the process of assessing the risks, consider each area of uncertainty in turn. An obvious starting point is the relationship with and/or the reputation of the client. This might be followed by considering whether the available information is adequate to provide a proper basis for a bid, i.e. definition of the commission, the scope of the services and any conditions relating to the fee itself.

"The fee should be based on an analysis of the benefits and risks to the practice"

The assessment of risks at inception should be part of the risk management procedures which apply to the business in general and at all stages of a commission.

The client

If the client is a registered company, check:

- its financial status with Dunn and Bradstreet or a similar credit-referencing firm
- its website, and
- its annual accounts.

If the client is a UK plc, try www.paymentscorer.com – a joint venture between the Federation of Small Businesses, The Credit Management Research Centre and The Better Payment Practice Group, which gives payment league tables. Several banks now also provide a credit-checking service to small businesses.

If the client is a subsidiary company in a larger group, consider whether a parental guarantee should be obtained.

Making a check on other clients is more difficult; try other local architects, contractors or business contacts.

Do not engage with a client if you are uncomfortable about any aspect of the commission. If possible, identify the person who makes decisions, gives instruction and signs cheques, and also any interested third parties.

Defining the commission

Before deciding to make a fee offer, consider the three vital elements – services, targets and the terms – and the following questions.

The services

- What services are required or requested? Will they be adequate and deliverable?
- Are there any risks or uncertainties in the description of the services? Are they manageable? Should they be classified as 'additional services'?
- Will the procurement route affect the services or the programme for their delivery?
- Are the roles of lead consultant, lead designer, contract administrator (or equivalent) included?
- Are any of the services beyond the practice's experience or resources? If so, how will they be provided? Will it be necessary to retain sub-consultants?
- Are other consultants to be appointed?
- Are there opportunities for added value?

Targets

- If a target programme is given, is it reasonable?
- If a target cost is given, does it include fees, VAT and other costs, and/or is it reasonable?
- Are there any other factors which might affect delivery of the project – for example, the stability of economic conditions in the market-place (see Section 7), or dependence on and certainty of external approvals or funding?

Terms and conditions for the offer

The terms and conditions of the proposed agreement with the client and client requirements which affect the fee offer itself are equally important issues.

- Will the agreement be made using a RIBA document or, if not, are the terms comprehensive and in writing?
- Does the client understand the payment provisions?
- Will the appointment be for all stages or just one stage at a time?
- Are the terms reasonable and insurable?
- Is extra or special professional indemnity (PI) insurance cover necessary?

Whether or not the fee is competitive, only an appropriate and carefully con-sidered fee will adequately reimburse the architect for the performance of the services so that the client can be assured that the necessary resources to deliver the project can be afforded. On the other hand, it is important to remember that the fee is the cost to the client of buying the architect's services.

Beware of any requirement to state the ultimate total fee (or maximum price) unless the bases of the estimate – the services – are clearly specified and there is provision for additional fees for additional services.

If the offer is required to include an estimate of the total fee expenditure, indicate clearly that it is only an approximate estimate and that actual fees will reflect the services provided. Also, after appointment, make certain that any change is notified promptly, although this principle applies whether or not fees are affected.

The decision to make a fee offer

If the analysis of the benefits and risks supports a decision to make an offer, as a final check, consider the following questions:

- Are you comfortable about working with this client?
- Are the client's requirements firm or just aspirations, and what are the chances of changes being introduced from the starting point?
- Do you have sufficient information about the services and your roles?

Specimen letter confirming commission for preliminary services

IVOR B'ARCH Architects LLP

Prospect Drive Thawbridge BS17 2ZX

T: 0100 012 023
F: 0100 012 024
E: ivor@b'arch.com

RIBA ♯♯
Chartered Practice

Toymakers Ltd   17 September 20XX
2 The Green
Barset BS3 6QG   Our ref: 412/IB/002

For the attention of Mr Eric Blyton

Dear Mr Blyton

Redevelopment of 2 The Green, Barset

We write to confirm that you have asked us to perform some preliminary services in connection with this project and to confirm the terms of our appointment.

You have explained your objectives and asked us to:

1 carry out some feasibility studies for the project – in particular to identify solutions (a) to re-provide accommodation for your business and (b) to maximise the use of the site;

2 to prepare the design brief on your behalf.

For the above services to be provided effectively, you have agreed we shall act as lead consultant and lead designer and you will appoint structural and building services engineers and a quantity surveyor to assist us.

You have commissioned a measured survey of the site and we noted that it may also be necessary to commission surveys of the existing services and the ground conditions.

Performance of our services will be charged on a time basis. Time-based services are charged at the following rates:

Principal £100 per hour   Associate £75 per hour

Senior architect £55 per hour   Architect £50 per hour

Technician £43 per hour

In addition, we shall invoice you for our expenses, including printing, reproduction and travelling costs and any disbursements made on your behalf. Accounts will be submitted monthly. (Value added tax, where applicable, is chargeable on the net value of our fees and expenses.)

We will perform the services in accordance with the RIBA Standard Conditions for the Appointment of an Architect, a copy of which is enclosed. We shall, of course, review progress with you regularly and advise you of the options for development.

We should like to propose the use of the Master Planning schedule for our services and for other consultants, which will allow the team to co-ordinate its activities. We have marked the activities which we think are appropriate and can co-ordinate these with the other consultants at the first team meeting.

We envisage that this preliminary appointment will continue for approximately __ weeks. During this period we can discuss the further services required to complete the project and the detailed terms of our agreement. When the agreement has been entered into, this preliminary appointment will be subsumed into it, and fees invoiced under this letter will rank as payments on account.

If you agree that this is a correct summary of your requirements, please sign the enclosed copy of this letter and return it to us. We shall then be in a position to start work. We are looking forward to working with you on this project.

Yours faithfully

Ivor B'Arch

for and on behalf of Ivor B'Arch Architects LLP

I confirm that Ivor B'Arch Architects LLP are to proceed with the preliminary services as set out above.

signed *Eric Blyton* for *Toymakers Ltd* [date] *2nd October 20XX*

Section 3
Work stage fees and the procurement route

In this Section:

- *Work stage fees*
- *RIBA Outline Plan of Work 2007*
- *Division of the fee by work stage*
- *Normal services*
- *Other services*
- *Services and the procurement route*

> *Only architects can get the brief defined, get a concept set down and get planning permission for it. This is where we are most valuable and should not be giving work away. After this our uniqueness fades. Yet the majority of fees come from the later stages. We under-sell our high-value work and oversell our lower value efforts.*
>
> Richard Saxon, *Building Design*, 26 November 2004

Work stage fees

Work stage fees can be the first step in planning cash flow to the benefit of both client and architect.

See also:
Periodic
payments,
page 62

They engage both parties in the progressive development of the cost of the project, avoiding surprise 'creep' and allowing for review of briefing or design decisions affecting the cost of construction (and the fee).

Where the fee is percentage based – the traditional or the variable lump sum options – work stage fees create a fair balance of the risks, add transparency to the operation and bring an element of value management into the process.

Neither party obtains a windfall as a result of inflation or deflation in the cost of construction.

RIBA Outline Plan of Work 2007

The RIBA Outline Plan of Work 2007 (amended November 2008), which describes the RIBA Work Stages, is detailed in Figure 3.1, and diagrams showing RIBA Work Stage sequences by procurement method are given in Figure 3.2.

Division of the fee by work stage

Although no recent survey has been carried out to indicate how fees relate to work stages, early guidance on work stage allocations remains a useful adjunct to empirically defined fees and a handy check for resource-based fees.

However, the way in which payment of the fee for 'normal' services – the basic fee – is to be spread across the anticipated programme is a matter of judgement, which will be influenced by the nature of the project, by commercial considerations and/or by the resource requirements. Whatever the decision, the fee offer should identify the proportion of the whole that is allocated to each work stage or group of work stages.

Where the appointment will be (or there is a risk that it may be) made stage by stage, the fee offer for each stage should be discrete and reflect its real value.

Table 3.1 shows the historic division of the basic fee for normal services applied to RIBA 2007 Work Stages, reflecting the 'added value' of the concept stages. Table 3.2 shows division of the basic fee for normal services applied to the RIBA Schedule of Services for a Small Project, where some of the stages are combined (see page 24).

'Normal' services

The architect's 'normal' services for traditional procurement comprise management and design responsibilities. The management roles, apart from self-management, include the architect as lead designer, as lead consultant and as administrator of the building contract. These management services make the architect the primary contact with the client, and give authority and responsibility to the architect as the leader and co-ordinator of other designers. Performance of

The Outline Plan of Work organises the process of managing, and designing building projects and administering building contracts into a number of key Work Stages. The sequence or content of Work Stages may vary or they may overlap to suit the procurement method (see pages 2 and 3).

RIBA Work Stages		Description of key tasks	OGC Gateways
Preparation	A Appraisal	Identification of client's needs and objectives, business case and possible constraints on development. Preparation of feasibility studies and assessment of options to enable the client to decide whether to proceed.	**1** Business justification
Preparation	B Design Brief	Development of initial statement of requirements into the Design Brief by or on behalf of the client confirming key requirements and constraints. Identification of procurement method, procedures, organisational structure and range of consultants and others to be engaged for the project.	**2** Procurement strategy
Design	C Concept	Implementation of Design Brief and preparation of additional data. Preparation of Concept Design including outline proposals for structural and building services systems, outline specifications and preliminary cost plan. Review of procurement route.	**3A** Design Brief and Concept Approval
Design	D Design Development	Development of concept design to include structural and building services systems, updated outline specifications and cost plan. Completion of Project Brief. *Application for detailed planning permission.*	
Design	E Technical Design	Preparation of technical design(s) and specifications, sufficient to co-ordinate components and elements of the project and *information for statutory standards and construction safety.*	**3B** Detailed Design Approval
Pre-Construction	F Production Information	F1 Preparation of production information in sufficient detail to enable a tender or tenders to be obtained. *Application for statutory approvals.* F2 *Preparation of further information for construction required under the building contract.*	
Pre-Construction	G Tender Documentation	*Preparation and/or collation of tender documentation in sufficient detail to enable a tender or tenders to be obtained for the project.*	
Pre-Construction	H Tender Action	*Identification and evaluation of potential contractors and/or specialists for the project. Obtaining and appraising tenders; submission of recommendations to the client.*	**3C** Investment decision
Construction	J Mobilisation	Letting the building contract, appointing the contractor. Issuing of information to the contractor. Arranging site hand over to the contractor.	
Construction	K Construction to Practical Completion	Administration of the building contract to Practical Completion. Provision to the contractor of further Information as and when reasonably required. Review of information provided by contractors and specialists.	**4** Readiness for Service
Use	L Post Practical Completion	L1 Administration of the building contract after Practical Completion and making final inspections. L2 Assisting building user during initial occupation period. L3 Review of project performance in use.	**5** Benefits evaluation

The activities in *italics* may be moved to suit project requirements, ie:
D   *Application for detailed planning approval;*
E   *Statutory standards and construction safety;*
F1 *Application for statutory approvals;* and
F2 *Further information for construction.*
G+H *Invitation and appraisal of tenders*

FIGURE 3.1: *RIBA Outline Plan of Work 2007 (amended November 2008)*

The diagrams illustrate different sequences for completion of work stages for various procurement methods, but are not representative of time.
In arriving at an acceptable timescale the choice of procurement method may be as relevant as other more obvious factors such as the amount of work to be done, the client's tendering requirements, risks associated with third party approvals or funding etc.
✛ This symbol indicates that prior to commencement time should be allowed for appointing consultants.

Fully designed project single stage tender

Select advisors	✛ A B		Planning					
Select / confirm consultants	✛ C D E	F1		F2				L3
		G H	J	K		L1+2		

Fully designed project with design by contractor or specialist

Select advisors	✛ A B		Planning				
Select / confirm consultants	✛ C D E	F1		F2	F2		
Pre-contract design by Specialist	G* H*	F1	H2				
Post-contract design by Contractor or Specialist			F2			L3	
Competitive single stage tender		G H*	J	K		L1+2	
Two stage main contract tender	G* H*	F1	G H2				

G* First stage documentation, H* First stage tender may include Contractor's Proposals, H2 Second stage tender

Design and build project single stage tender

Select advisors	✛ A B		Planning	Design review		
Select / confirm consultants	✛ C D					L3
Employer's requirements		G	H	J	K	L1+2
Contractor's proposals		E		F		

Note: final design activity by Client may be at stage C, D, E or possibly F. These stages not repeated by contractor

Design and build project two stage tender (all design by contractor)

Appoint consultants	✛ A B		Design review			L3
Employer's requirements		G	H1	H2	J/K	L1+2
Contractor's proposals			C	D/E	F	
			Planning			

Partnering contract

Output specification by client

Appoint consultants	✛ A B		Planning			
Appoint partnering team		H C D E	F1	F2		
Select specialists		H E	F1	F2		L3
Agree guaranteed maximum price			G/H	J/K	L1+2	

Design and construction sequences may be as shown for Management contract/ Construction management

FIGURE 3.2: *RIBA Work Stage sequences by procurement method*

Management Contract / Construction Management

Select advisors ⊕ A B ☐ Planning

Select / confirm consultants ⊕ C D

Select MC or CM G H L2

J K L1+2

Shell and core packages E F1 G H F2 J K

Fit out packages E F1 G H F2

MC = management contractor CM = construction manager

Specialist contractors should be appointed by the management contractor or the construction manager as appropriate in time for the delivery of any pre-construction design services as required by the overall programme. Each package will require building control approval before its construction commences.

Public Private Partnerships and **Private Finance Initiative**

PPP/PFI stages

Preparation	Tenders/Negotiations	Construction	Use
1.1 Inception	2.1 First bids	3.1 Contract award	4 After hand-over
1.2 Pre-qualification	2.2 Second bids	3.2 Construction	5 Commissioning / operations
1.3 Output specification	2.3 Preferred bidder to financial close		6 Evaluation

OGC model 0 1 2 3.1 3.2 4 5

Negotiations / Brief review Compliance audit 5

Select client design advisors ⊕ 1.1 - 3 2.1 2.2 2.3 3 4 6

5

Provider's outputs 1.2 2.1 2.2 2.3 3 4 6

Provider's design team C D + E F1 F2 L1/2 L3

Planning

SMART PFI Variations

Select client design advisors ⊕ 1.3 1.3 review *Negotiations / Brief review* Compliance audit 5

Select / develop a design model Planning 4 6

5

Provider's outputs 1.2 2.1 /2 2.3 3 4 6

Provider's Design Team (D+) E F1 F2 - K L1/2 L3

RIBA stages

FIGURE 3.2: *Continued*

Note: The diagrams illustrate different sequences for completion of Work Stages for various procurement methods, but are not representative of time. In arriving at an acceptable time-scale the choice of that method may be as relevant as other, more obvious factors such as the amount of work to be done, the client's tendering requirements, risks associated with third-party approvals or funding, etc.

TABLE 3.1: *Work stage fees*

	RIBA Work Stage	Historical	Alternative
AB	Preparation	Time charges	
C	Concept	20%	35%
D	Design Development	20%	
E	Technical Design	15%	
F	Production Information	20%	35%
G	Tender Documentation	2%	
H	Tender Action	1%	
J	Mobilisation	1%	30% *includes F2*
K	Construction to Practical Completion	20%	
L	Post Practical Completion	1%	
		100%	100%

these services is demanding and requires the allocation of appropriate personnel and time for efficient delivery.

Where the management services are not to be performed by the architect, there will be consequential effects on the resources required and the concomitant fee for the architect's role purely as designer. Nevertheless, remember that the duties will include:

- collaboration and co-ordination with others, and integration into the architect's work of information received from them, and
- site inspection services during the construction period (relating only to the work designed by the architect).

TABLE 3.2: *Work stage fees for a small project*

	RIBA Work Stage	Fees
AB	Preparation	Time charges
CD	Design	35%
EFG	Construction information	35%
HJKL	Tender and construction	30%
		100%

Other services

Those services that are not always required or cannot reasonably be included in the basic fee for the normal services are called 'other services', which are usually charged on a time basis. A wide range of such services is shown in the services schedules to RIBA Agreements.

It is important therefore to identify, or at least consider, any such activities and identify the fee basis. Such activities may include negotiations with local authority planning and building control departments and any subsequent changes made to the submitted material, or dealing with contractor's claims.

Design stages C, D and E

Historically, it was common to weight the fee for the early design stages to reflect the architect's intellectual and conceptual skills, on which the success of the project depends.

> *Front-end loading is justified on the basis that the original intellectual input by architects occurs in the conceptual phase as they devise the solution to the client's brief. In addition, the 'added value' of securing planning permission should be rewarded by a payment that exceeds any time-based input.*
>
> Anne Minogue, *Building*, 2 February 2001

More recently, the downward pressure on fees by clients has moved many practitioners to reduce the fees for those stages closer to the resource costs. This is tantamount to denying the idea of 'added value', which originates in the concept stage.

Pre-construction stages F, G and H

In 1982 the RIBA recommended that allocation of the fee should be 35 per cent for Work Stages C and D, 40 per cent for Work Stages E, F and G and 25 per cent to completion. It was also noted that 'Fees in respect of Work Stages E to L should be paid in instalments proportionate to the work completed'. But, this advice was not followed, and complaints by architects that the proportion of the fee allocated to the construction stage was inadequate were common. This was largely a result of underestimating the extent of the work involved in co-ordinating and integrating design information from contractors or specialist sub-contractors, elaborating design details or preparing designs for work in provisional sums or measurements.

To address this problem, in 1998 RIBA Work Stage F (Production Information) was divided into two parts: preparation of the information necessary for obtaining tenders, and preparation of further production information required under the building contract.

It will be difficult to calculate the fee for each part, unless the division can be predicted with reasonable accuracy. If a single fee is selected for both parts, resources will need to be reserved until Work Stages J and K. RIBA Conditions of Appointment state that 'instalments of fees shall be calculated on the basis of the estimated percentage of completion'. In some circumstances it may be feasible to predetermine the fee for Work Stage F1, and charge F2 on a time basis.

Construction stages J, K and L1

For these stages, many architects charge on a time basis as progress and quality are governed by the contractor's performance (assuming the architect isn't also in default!). Such fees must be rigorously accounted for and exclude time spent in the preparation of further production information if the basic fee includes for Work Stage F2.

Services and the procurement route

Where the procurement method will not be a traditional lump sum building contract for a fully designed project, the services will be similar to the norm but delivered to different programmes, may exclude some work stages or, alternatively, may require a greater number of separate packages to be tendered and/or managed, as discussed below.

Design and build

Where a project is to be procured by the design and build method, the architect may be engaged for the preparation of the (Employer's) Requirements or for preparation of the (Contractor's) Proposals. Each requires different levels of input, which should be taken into account when estimating the resources required.

(Employer's) Requirements

Where the (Employer's) Requirements will comprise outline proposals and the performance specification only, the architect's work stages would be RIBA Work Stages A and/or C, G and H before appointment of the contractor. However, preparing the (Employer's) Requirements performance specification at Work Stage G might require more resources than a prescriptive specification in the absence of a detailed design basis, and Work Stage H includes appraisal of the (Contractor's) Proposals submitted with the tender.

If the client requires more control over the design or the architect is to be switched or novated (see below) to the contractor after tender stage, it is likely that the pre-tender stages would include at least Work Stage D and full planning approval.

The obligations and authority of the architect, if retained by the client as employer's agent during Work Stages J, K and L, are different to those of a contract administrator, but will include review and integration of any further information from the contractor.

(Contractor's) Proposals

For preparation of the (Contractor's) Proposals, where the (Employer's) Requirements provide minimal information, the contractor would appoint an architect for RIBA Work Stages C, G and H. After acceptance of the contractor client's tender, the Work Stages would be J, D, E, F and, perhaps, K and L.

Where the (Employer's) Requirements include a design with detailed planning permission, the Work Stages for the contractor's architect might be A, G and H. After acceptance of the contractor client's tender the Work Stages would be J, E, F, K and L.

Consultant switch or novation

Where the architect is to be switched to the contractor (i.e. the agreement with the architect is terminated concurrent with commencement of a new agreement with the contractor), terms and conditions and the fees to be paid by the contractor should be a contractual requirement, with provision for client intervention in the event of proposed termination of the architect's services by the contractor.

Where the architect is to be novated, the architect's agreement is maintained but the contractor becomes the client in lieu of the (now) employer.

In both cases, the fee offer should cover all stages and not be changed after initial acceptance, except, of course, for negotiated or necessary changes to the services.

Management contracts

In management contracting or construction management, the factors to consider will be the anticipated number of works or trade contracts, the extent of design by specialist contractors and the number of tender invitations. Where, for a moderate-sized project using traditional procurement, there may be one tender package sent to, say, four or five tenderers, in a substantial construction management project there may be 50 or more packages, each going to three or four tenderers.

These will not radically change the architect's design services from traditional procurement, but the overlapping of design, multiple package tendering, evaluating specialists' designs and the earlier start of construction will alter the extent, timing and use of resources. Of course, the architect's management duties and the resources required will also vary, particularly in the case of construction management.

Public–private partnerships and private finance initiative schemes

Apart from an appointment for the RIBA's Smart PFI client-led design stage, the architect will usually be appointed at the pre-qualification stage, either by the bidding consortium or special purpose vehicle (SPV) or by its contractor, and the terms and services required will be similar to an appointment by a contractor for (Contractor's) Proposals.

The most significant aspect is the discontinuous progress caused by the competitive rules of the game. Work stage names may be different or, particularly when financial close is reached, the services may be defined by a schedule of 'deliverables', i.e. specific drawing schedules, etc., and, after all the delays, in accordance with a demanding programme for their delivery. As the project progresses, and particularly at financial close, the sequence will closely resemble that of management contracts.

At the earliest stages, the provisional agreement with the SPV might be based on a letter similar to that for other speculative projects. There may also be an option to invest part of or the entire fee in the SPV as a speculative gesture.

The 'percentage ceiling' fee option is often favoured by many consortia.

The architect's role is seen as very important by the SPV (and the client) at the conceptual design stage. The wise architect will consider how best to secure the commission for the later stages or retain copyright of the design; for example, by requiring a substantial licence fee.

Section 4
Evaluating the resource cost

In this Section:

- *Choosing the evaluation method*
- *Empirical definition of the fee using historical data*
- *Calculating the resource requirements*
- *The margin*

A Client's Guide to Engaging an Architect (RIBA Publishing, November 2009) notes under 'Fee options':

> *In proposing a fee your architect will allow for the professional and financial resources required for your specific project and for your architect's conceptual skills and specialist knowledge, on which the success of the project will be based.*
>
> *Complex projects are likely to require the highest level of resources but larger projects may offer opportunity for efficiency savings.*

It also notes that fees will be influenced by:

- the extent of the architect's services and the type of procurement
- the size and complexity of the project and any project-specific requirements
- works to existing buildings (refurbishment and extensions) which are likely to be significantly more resource intensive
- the repair and conservation of historic buildings, which is even more complex and the fee proportionately higher
- repetition – for example, a number of houses or factory units to an identical design occurring on the original site; the Basic Fee may be adjusted in recognition of the reduced resources required

- if the design is to be repeated on other projects or sites – for instance, where a design for a house type is to be repeated by a contractor an additional fee may be payable.

An independent survey of average fees and hourly rates charged by architectural practices is published annually by the Fees Bureau (www.feesbureau.co.uk).

The *Business Benchmarking for RIBA Chartered Practices* report 2007/08 (see page 34) also includes some useful observations.

Choosing the evaluation method

There are three methods for evaluating the costs of providing the services. The first is to use empirical data. The second is to predict the time and resources required and calculate their probable cost. The third, and probably safest method, uses the second method and checks the result against the first.

"If the architect cannot afford to perform the contracted services the client also suffers and, to compound the injury, there may be a claim for the client's consequential losses"

If the client's brief leaves too much to the imagination, and the architect's response is based around a published percentage, perhaps adding something to cover risk, but more likely deducting something to get the work, the consequences can be painful.

In the past, this optimistic, even sloppy, approach has led to the demise of several practices, some very well-known, who were unlucky enough to have secured commissions without an adequate examination of the costs. It might be noted that if the architect cannot afford to perform the contracted services the client also suffers and, to compound the injury, there may be a claim for the client's consequential losses.

Empirical definition of the fee using historical data

In 1982 the Monopolies Commission, and in 2002 the Office of Fair Trading (OFT), required the RIBA (and other professional institutions) to abandon any guidance that might be construed as 'recommended fees'. Many, perhaps most, architects used the empirical option, i.e. drawing on published data, personal experience and/or any available historical data to establish a percentage fee applicable to the building type for the 'normal' services or, if necessary, an equivalent lump sum.

For some time, clients have been becoming more demanding, a process which has included a move away from percentage fees, although they are used extensively as a benchmark by both clients and consultants. In an uncertain world, they provide a reasonable indication of what one might expect to pay, although they are sometimes translated into lump sums once the extent of work required is clearly defined. However, the advent of competitive bidding and the common requirement for lump sum fees demands a proper brief from the client and careful consideration of the risks.

M. Paul Nicholson in the *Architects' Guide to Fee Bidding* (Spon Press, 2002) demonstrates how some additional calculations may be used to arrive at an empirical fee that is more reflective of the project than the common method described above. Whether the extra calculations will be adequate to cover the risks or ensure a profit is another matter of judgement when using the empirical method.

If this empirical method is used, it would be wise to check whether:

- the fee will provide adequate time – by dividing the fee, less the margin, by the average hourly cost, and
- the work stage allocations are appropriate.

Historical data

Practice records, for which a number of management software packages with different degrees of sophistication are available, are the best source of data when assembling a new fee offer. Records might show details of each commission by building type, and of time spent by each individual with their grade or salary, together with an analysis of profit (or loss). The usefulness of the data is enhanced where the records are on a stage-by-stage basis.

The Building Cost Information Service (BCIS) issues a quarterly review of the construction costs of most building types, classified using the CI/Sfb system and based on tender price analyses. Such information could be a vital element where the client has not specified a target cost for the project.

Note that the regional variation in fee levels as reported by the Fees Bureau is very similar to the regional variation in cost of construction as reported by the BCIS.

Consider also the key performance indicators sponsored by Constructing Excellence (www.constructingexcellence.org.uk) or the benchmarking services of a management consultant such as Colander (www.colander.co.uk).

Business Benchmarking for RIBA Chartered Practices

The 2007/08 report prepared by Colander and MRM makes some very interesting observations on the business attitudes of the responding practices, including the following extracts.

> **Efficiency**   *[A] useful tool for businesses is a measure of efficiency that compares actual income to capacity – capacity being the number of fee earners × their charge out rates × their targeted number of chargeable hours. It is therefore disappointing to see that only a quarter of the practices in this survey bother to set targeted chargeable hours for their fee earners which suggests that few practices are able to accurately gauge actual versus potential income.*
>
> **Monitoring time**   *[A] quarter of the practices in this survey do not require all fee-earners to submit time sheets, nor do they measure or allocate their non-chargeable time to different activities. Without comprehensive and accurate time sheets it is nigh on impossible to monitor how much time – and therefore how much money – it takes to perform each project stage, or to run each aspect of the business. It goes without saying that it is difficult also to plan effectively on new projects or when contemplating a change of direction for the practice itself.*
>
> *As with other financial measures, it is the smaller practices that are most lax when it comes to monitoring their use of time. However, it is sobering to realise that 14% of the larger practices are also without accurate time measurements.*
>
> **Hours worked**   *Assuming a normal 37.5 hour week, there are around 1,760 working hours in a year, once holidays and sickness have been taken into account.*
>
> *If the figures submitted by practices in this survey are to be believed, then the folklore that architects work ridiculously long hours is not correct. Across the survey, the more junior people are averaging only a few hours a year more than this standard and, while the number of hours rises with seniority, equity partners and shareholder directors are averaging less than 250 hours a year more, or around an hour a day. That said, from the most senior person to the most junior, people who work for larger*

practices are working longer hours, with people in London working the longest hours of all – across the board.

The question is how many of those hours are chargeable to clients?

One would expect the junior ranks to be close to 100% chargeable, so it is disappointing to see averages of 85% to 87% for architects, technologists and architectural assistants. These percentages rise slightly for large practices and for London based practices. However, there is clearly room for improved levels of efficiency in the junior ranks, which probably needs to be driven by improved management skills at senior levels.

Fee arrangements *Following the trend of recent years, percentage-based fees account for a diminishing proportion of fees, averaging in this survey, only just over 40% of all fees. Importantly, fixed fees equally account for 40% of all fees, highlighting the need for practices to be acutely aware of how much it costs to undertake each stage of each project as well as the overall cost of running their businesses.*

Charge out rates *Charge out rates vary enormously across the survey. However, it is interesting to see that the largest discrepancies appear to be at senior level; while for more junior staff the distinctions are much less startling.*

Interestingly, in the middle and lower ranks the figures are much more comparable, with variances of only a few pounds between rates. This suggests that smaller practices could, and perhaps should, value their part-ners' time much more highly, especially since they will find themselves competing against their larger rivals on certain projects.

On average, London practices work to higher charge out rates at all levels of seniority and, again, this is most marked at senior level, where the lowest rates in London are higher than the highest rates in the regions – but even at more junior levels, regional highs and London lows are comparable.

Bearing in mind that many London practices operate very profitably across the nation, and in competition with regional practices, it is worth considering what drives their success – it is presumably not a result of low fees.

Calculating the resource requirements

Calculating the fee from the cost of the estimated resource requirements is an alternative to the empirical method. It will also provide valuable input to the historical database, which is a vital part of the practice's self-knowledge.

The data required to calculate the fee includes the outputs or tasks, the time they will take, the staff available and the cost, as discussed in Appendix D (page 101). The resource requirements in terms of personnel can be defined by their activities; the major activity is preparing (and developing or revising) drawings and related information, for which preliminary schedules can be drawn up, but the management and administrative tasks will also take time.

The steps before calculating a fee, perhaps using a spreadsheet system similar to that illustrated in Appendix D, will include:

- provisionally allocating professionals and technologists to reflect the quality of service required and the competence of the people involved and checking against the practice's workload programme
- drawing up a provisional schedule of activities and time requirements
- calculating the real cost of the staff required
- identifying any ancillary costs, such as travel, additional PI insurance cover, hardware or software requirements
- identifying the margin appropriate for the commission
- defining the fee (see Section 5).

The margin

Whether using the empirical method or calculating the resources, attention must be given to what is sometimes referred to as the 'margin', or the difference between:

- the direct costs of employment of each fee earner, i.e. the direct payroll costs, employer's National Insurance contributions and benefits such as car allowances, pension contributions, life and health insurance, professional subscriptions, CPD programmes and recruitment, and
- the indirect costs, i.e. the overhead costs, including such items as working capital and premises, and enough profit to be reinvested in the growth and development of the practice.

Both the planned and the actual margin will vary between one commission and the next, depending on any number of factors. Some protection can be built in to the fee offer for obvious risks, by choosing the calculated lump sum option, including a contingency provision, increasing the margin or including an allowance for inflation where no provision is made in the conditions.

Alternatively, a low margin may be an element of the bid – for instance, because the practice needs the commission or as a lead into other commissions with the client. Although the profitability of the practice as a whole is what counts at the end of the day, the aim should be that each commission will contribute its share.

It is also important to consider how any provisions for 'added value' may impact on the margin.

Setting the margin is therefore a matter of practical politics. However, the consequences of accepting a commission at a price which the practice cannot afford may have much more serious implications than the low fee.

> *Bearing in mind that many London practices operate very profitably across the nation, and in competition with regional practices, it is worth considering what drives their success – it is presumably not a result of low fees.*
> *Business Benchmarking for RIBA Chartered Practices* (see page 34)

The simple system demonstrated in Figure C.4 (page 100) includes both direct and indirect elements in the calculation of the hourly rate for each fee-earner. For larger practices it may be more appropriate to calculate the direct costs first and make a separate decision about the marginal costs for each project.

There is also some risk that the insurer might deny cover for non-negligent liability, if the fee is so low that the architect cannot afford the resources required or the practice is under-funded.

Other things to remember

- ARB Code Standard 2 requires architects to 'provide adequate professional, financial and technical competence and resources'.
- ARB Code Standard 11 requires that 'the fee or the method of calculating it' shall have been recorded in writing before any professional work is undertaken.
- CDM Regulations require the allocation of adequate time and resources by persons with duties under the regulations.
- The offer must provide a reasonable commercial return to the architect's practice.
- In accepting an appointment the architect offers to perform services 'as specialist' (*R. v. Architects' Registration Tribunal, ex p. Jaggar* [1945] 2 All ER 131),

the fee should therefore be adequate to meet all the obligations 'as specialist' and the risks arising, as well as achieving the desired profit. However, the architect 'specialist' should avoid claiming to act as 'expert'.

- The more complex the project the more data is required for design development in Work Stages C and D.
- If the client or the practice requires additional PI insurance cover for the project, it is essential to determine how it will be financed.

Section 5
Defining the fee

In this Section:

- *Valuing your work*
- *Betterment or incentive fees*
- *Equity shares*
- *Value framework*
- *The traditional options*
- *Other options*
- *Expenses*
- *Presentation*

> *When invited to quote for architectural or other services, members should ensure that they have sufficient information about the commission for the calculation of their fee. Any fee quotation should clearly indicate the type and extent of the services (a defined scope of works) to be undertaken for that fee, and will also enable any subsequent changes to be identified. **Members should ensure that they have adequate and appropriate financial and technical resources and professional expertise to deliver the services offered.***
>
> *RIBA Code of Professional Conduct 2005:*
> *Guidance Note 4 – Appointments*

This section examines various methods available for defining the way in which fees and expenses will be charged to the client, taking into account the benefits, risks and costs of the potential commission.

The component parts of such fees will be:

- the Basic Fee for performing the architect's normal services, as set out in the agreement with the client, plus

- any fee for Other Services
- provision for time charges, and
- expenses (see page 48).

The Basic Fee will usually exclude the fee for any separately identified 'Other Services' and should identify the chosen method of calculation and the percentages or lump sums. Indication of how the fee will be apportioned for each stage or group of stages will prove beneficial if changes are made subsequently to the cost or programme.

If performance of multiple roles is required, such as architect as designer, lead consultant, lead designer, contract administrator, or, say, access management specialist, consider whether the fee for any of these roles should be charged separately.

Note that in RIBA Agreements provision is made for annual review of fixed lump sums and time charges, for additional fees and for interest on late payments. The Average Earnings Index and the Consumer Prices Index are published by the Office for National Statistics (www.statistics.gov.uk).

Identify the fee for any specified Other Service or, if applicable, state that it is included in the Basic Fee. Give details if an 'other agreed method' has been chosen.

Valuing your work

The first consideration must be the value the practice puts on its own work.

> *In my view, it is ourselves that give us this low self-esteem and keep us at the bottom end of the professional earnings scale. We need to convince clients of our great value and benefits to them – not just lament the competition and free-market we all live in.*
>
> Richard Brindley, RIBAnet, 17 July 2006

Draw up a list of other milestones demonstrating value achievements. These are the basis of betterment or incentive fees, equity shares or a value framework.

Obviously, with such methods, which are based on uncertain outcomes, there will be a risk of 'no success, no reward' and counterclaims for poor performance. Generally, these options will be proposed or required by the client, but there is no reason why any of these methods should not be proposed by architects with appropriate entrepreneurial skills (or compulsive gamblers). Whichever option is adopted, clarity and accuracy are paramount.

Architects who are sure that the quality of their design and their standards of performance always add value should not be risk averse.

"Architects ... should not be risk averse"

Betterment or incentive fees

A betterment or incentive fee, usually additional to the basic fee, might be agreed for rewarding achievement of cost savings, reduction in energy consumption, lower through-life costs for the project or other stated aims such as planning gain.

The parameters for such rewards would include the baseline from which the benefits would be measured, the nature of the reward and the timing of the payment. The baseline might be, for instance:

* the estimates for the targeted capital or revenue costs made as part of the submission of the detailed design proposals for approval (at the end of RIBA Work Stage D), or
* the value of the site or property before planning permission.

In the latter case, the reward should become payable on the grant of permission, but in the former case payment would probably be deferred until twelve months after practical completion so that the cost benefits can be calculated from the agreed final account and/or actual revenue costs. Depending on the nature of the target achievements, the additional fee might be a percentage or a sliding scale of lump sums to reflect, say, 50 per cent of the architect's net contribution to the benefits. The terms of such arrangements should be very carefully drafted, and for complex deals perhaps with advice from a lawyer.

Equity shares

The architect may agree or offer to accept equity shares in a project in exchange for carrying some of the financial risks if the finances of the practice could support the inevitable deferment of any return. Such a scheme must be arranged with the help of the practice's legal advisor.

Value framework

At the RIBA Conference, Facing the Future, 2002, Roger Zogolovitch proposed that the fee for projects built for sale, lease or rental might be based on profitability. The proposal is developer-led and has repercussions on the architect's (and other consultants') design and construction processes. The methodology described below could be adapted for other projects where the client has experience of other construction projects.

> A 'value framework' [has] three key indicators – project value, project cost, project margin:
> * project value *is the gross value of the net floor area comprised in the project*
> * project cost *is the best estimate of the cost of construction to complete the project*
> * project margin *is the difference between project value and project cost.*

The value framework process:

* at RIBA Work Stages A and B prepare and evaluate the proposed project value – project cost and project margin
* architect and client agree on the range of values – rates per m² of net floor area by use
* the project cost target is established – by reference to the current floor area
* the project margin is the agreed difference between the forecast cost and value
* the design team (all project professionals) agree to conform to the value framework
* the fees are agreed on the traditional basis fee and converted to a fixed percentage of the project margin – this percentage is applied throughout the job.

The traditional options

Percentage fees

This traditional option is to express the fee as a percentage of the final cost of construction. This option is most appropriate for straightforward building projects of relatively short duration where normal services are required and the details of the project, its cost and programme are defined at the beginning. Surveys, feasibility studies, developing the initial brief, etc. would normally involve additional time charges.

Once upon a time, an architect would absorb all the unexpected costs arising in the performance of the services, for example variations, claims, etc., in return for the percentage fee on the total out-turn cost to the client. It was, therefore, one of the most convenient and easily understood methods of charging, although somewhat rough and ready.

This approach is generally no longer suited to current business methods of architects or clients. The method is open to the insinuation implicit in 'the higher the cost, the higher the fee'.

However, if the unexpected occurs – for instance, a substantial increase in the building cost – the consequential increase in the fee may give rise to difficult discussions with the client. Conversely, a decrease in the building cost because of market conditions at the date of the tender may mean that the architect has already drawn down all or most of the total fee and will still have to perform the construction stage services.

See also: The effect of market conditions, page 64

Lump sum fees

Some clients may prefer, for reasons of apparently greater certainty, to agree a lump sum or sums for the services. It is always desirable to agree such lump sums separately for each work stage, although a single lump sum may be divided into appropriate proportions (see page 24) with each section payable on completion of the relevant stage.

Fixed lump sums

Where the scope of the project, the services required, the programme and cost are clearly defined from the outset, and are likely to remain reasonably stable, fixed lump sums may be predetermined. However, except in the case of a highly focused service to be undertaken over a very short period, it is unwise to agree a fixed sum with no provision for variation. At the very least, provision should be made for such lump sum(s) to be varied if either of the parameters for time or cost change by more than, say, 10 per cent.

Calculated or variable lump sums

If change is likely, because of uncertainty in the brief, the programme, the cost or the client's aspirations, it may be appropriate to choose a method that can be used to calculate lump sums when the project has been sufficiently developed to remove those uncertainties. The lump sums are calculated by applying percentages for each work stage to the relevant cost of construction.

There are two options for the timing of making the calculations:

A   when the design is ready for submission for detailed planning approval, e.g. on completion of RIBA Work Stage D, or

B   more flexibly, at the beginning of each work stage based on the estimated cost of construction at the end of the previous stage. The fee for RIBA Work Stage C might be based provisionally on the budget at commencement until a realistic estimate is available.

If the client requires changes to the project which occur after a lump sum for a work stage has been calculated, these are treated as additional services.

Option B engages both client and architect in the progressive development of the cost of the project, avoiding surprise 'creep' and allowing for review of briefing or design decisions affecting the cost of construction (and the fee). Neither party obtains a windfall as a result of inflation or deflation in the cost of construction.

It creates a fair balance of the risks, adds transparency to the operation of the percentage fee method and brings an element of value management into the process.

Time charges

When the resources or the time-scale necessary for performance of the services cannot be predicted with reasonable accuracy, time charges will form the best and fairest basis for reimbursement. This is particularly relevant to RIBA Work Stages A and B. The time expended on the relevant services by principals, professional and technical staff is charged at agreed rates, usually expressed as hourly rates.

Whether or not this option is used for the basic fee, always agree rates for appropriate categories of staff and/or for named individuals, as it may also be necessary to have agreed rates in place should additional services or extra work become necessary. Provision should be made for revision of the rates for inflation/ deflation at, say, twelve-monthly intervals, and particularly where services will be provided over several years.

It is essential that accurate records of all time spent by principals, professional, technical and administrative staff are maintained for each commission, whether or not it is to be charged to the client. The information will be part of the historical data required for the next fee proposal, and may also be used as evidence if a claim is challenged by the client.

Time spent by professional and technical staff travelling in conjunction with time-charged services should be chargeable. It may sometimes be appropriate to charge the time of non-technical staff as a direct project cost, such as special research and secretarial back-up or computer time, but more often such time cannot be allocated in this way, and in any case this is a matter that should be agreed with the client.

Wherever time charges are employed, in the interests of both client and architect it may be beneficial to agree a provisional budget for the relevant service, work stage or change instruction. The 'percentage ceiling' option (see below) might be an alternative.

In an interesting development of this option, it was reported that the European Commission and the Architects Council of Europe were considering implementing a system based on the time taken to design a building. This is a fascinating development of the time-charged method, provided that the necessary data is forthcoming and acceptable to clients and construction professionals. However, when M. Paul Nicholson asked 24 practices to estimate the number of drawings that would be required for the design of a specific project, the answers ranged from 96 to 189 – a difference of almost 100 per cent!

Other options

'Percentage ceiling' fees

In this system the architect proceeds on a time basis but, if the total fee would exceed an agreed percentage, the latter is applied. The system gives a sort of *'maximum price'* relating to the ultimate cost and is favoured by consortia bidding for public–private partnership (PPP) projects. If the hourly rate applies, the consortia client gains and the architect does not lose, provided that the time charge rates are realistic and include an appropriate margin.

The system does not provide for additional instructions generating extra fees. There is, therefore, a danger that risks may arise if the purchaser's brief is inadequate, and/or consultations during the design process are used to sort out basic problems, and/or the designers, who may include specialist sub-contractors, do not develop team-working skills. The rates will need to be high enough to cover such risks. It should also be remembered that time charges will not compensate for the front-loading of the fee to reflect the architect's conceptual skills.

Unit price fees and fees for repetition

When the project is, or substantial parts of it are, plainly repetitive, fees may be agreed on a unit price – for example, on the number of hotel rooms, or per house type, etc. The unit price is effectively a form of lump sum. It may also be the basis for a royalty payment for the licence to copy a design on other sites. When a design is to be used on another site or repeated without the involvement of the original architect – for instance, if a house type is to be repeated by a contractor on various sites – it might be appropriate to agree a licence fee for the use of the architect's work for each house type.

Where the repetition, i.e. of a number of houses or factory units to an identical design, will occur on the original site, it may be appropriate to adjust the basic fee. The repetitive element, which will occur primarily in RIBA Work Stages E, F and G, might be acknowledged in setting the fee for those stages at a level that recognises the reduced resources required by the architect.

However, as the extent of repetition might be unknown when agreeing the fee, a formulaic basis to give a credit might be more appropriate.

The offer might be expressed as:

£ Credit for repeated design of [houses] [flats] [hotel rooms]
excluding [substructures] [any shared construction] or [installations]

$$= \frac{(\text{No. of units less one}) \times \text{unit cost}}{(\text{Cost of construction})}$$

$\times$ (X% of fee in £ for Work Stages E, F and G)

The fee for the relevant stages will be either the percentage fee for those work stages, or the proportion of the lump sum relating to the repeated design. The percentage reduction or rebate of the basic fee should take into account the fact that, although the design may be 'standard', it may have to be shown/repeated on location drawings. The formula also accommodates lump sum fees.

The unit is the *repeated design*, for example:

- the superstructure of detached houses
- the superstructure of terraced houses, excluding party walls
- flats, excluding all shared elements such as structure, external walls, roofs, services distribution systems, etc., or
- the fit-out elements of individual compartments such as hotel rooms.

For example, if:

- the cost of construction is £1,000,000
- there are 20 identical units estimated to cost £40,000 each
- the basic fee is 6 per cent of the cost of construction, of which 15 per cent is for Work Stage E, 20 per cent for F and 2 per cent for G
- and it has been decided to rebate 75 per cent of the fee for the identical units for Work Stages E, F and G

the calculation would be:

$$\frac{(20-1) \times 40,000}{1,000,000} \times (6\% \times £1,000,000 \times 37\% \times 75\%)$$

$$= \frac{760,000}{1,000,000} \times (£60,000 \times 37\% \times 75\%) = 0.76 \times £16,650 = £12,654 \text{ credit}$$

Licence fees

Whether or not the agreement explicitly says so, the client will have a right to use the architect's work for its intended purpose, for example to construct a building on the identified site, provided that the work has been paid for.

However, if the commission is in any way speculative or at risk from external influence, for instance in respect of financing or planning, or it is possible that the client, having obtained the benefit of planning approval, may decide to sell the site or to use the design-and-build approach, the fee offer for the first stage(s) might include an additional premium payment or licence fee for using the work, which would become payable if the architect is not appointed to perform further services.

Where it is known that the work will be used for other projects – for example, producing designs for a house builder – a licence fee or royalty for each use should be considered. The amount of that fee will not usually be very significant, although it should include an 'added-value' element.

Expenses

Expenses incurred on the commission may be:

- reimbursed at net cost, perhaps with the addition of a handling charge
- reimbursed by a percentage addition to the gross fee
- reimbursed by a fixed lump sum, or
- covered by the basic fee.

The first option does not require any explanation, but does involve considerable administrative time in collating the evidence and scheduling. It incurs no risk, unless the client wishes each item to be validated.

The percentage addition option is simple to operate, provided that it is clear which expenses are covered. The percentage can be calculated annually by expressing all relevant expenditure in the practice's accounts as a proportion of fee income. The data will also be required in the business planning reviews and as part of the historical data archive.

The fixed lump sum is also easy to operate, but the risks are carried by the architect.

If expenses are to be covered by the basic fee, the calculations must include an appropriate percentage addition.

Whichever option is chosen, specify which categories are to be covered; typically, these will include reproduction or purchase costs of documents, drawings, etc., photography and travel.

Specify different rates for reproduction of drawings and documents – for example, as black-and-white prints or as drawing files in electronic format.

'Drawings and documents' would include those used in communication between architect, client, consultants and contractors, and for enquiries or tenders, and also covers maps and photographs and printed forms of contract. Note that contractors should be asked to pay for any copies additional to those that they are entitled to under the building contract.

The agreement should make it clear that reimbursement will be due for any expenses not covered by the specified categories if the client's prior approval has been obtained, and for any disbursements made on the client's behalf; a handling charge for such expenditure to cover administration costs may also be appropriate.

To complete the arrangements, provision might also be made for recording mileage rates, and rates for in-house printing and plotting.

It is also essential that the architect maintains records of any expenses to be reimbursed, whether at net cost or otherwise, for the same reasons as maintaining time records, i.e. as part of the historical data required for the next fee proposal or, regrettably, as evidence if reimbursement is challenged by the client.

If the client requires the architect to incur particular costs, for instance to run and staff an office at the client's premises or to use specified computer software, consideration should be given to how these will be charged and the implications in the event of a change to the timetable, suspension or termination and decisions recorded in the fee offer.

Presentation

This part is about preparing the presentation to the client of the architect's proposals in their widest context.

First, consider the requirements for the presentation:

- Is the offer to be submitted prior to interview?
- Is the offer made in competition?
- Who will influence the decision to accept an offer, what are their roles?
- Which factors will add value to the client and/or the project?
- Which fee option is most likely to be acceptable?
- What information has the client requested with the offer, and/or what other information does the client need to know?

The offer should identify the components and make-up of the fee. It should refer to the available brief for the project on which the services to be provided are based, and to the conditions of appointment that will apply.

The information about the fee itself is most easily conveyed using a fee management schedule, as shown in Figure D.6 on page 112, or the RIBA Schedule of Fees and Expenses, as shown in Figure D.7 on page 113.

See also:
Appendix D,
page 101;
Appendix E,
page 117
A fee management schedule created by the resource system described in Appendix D can be linked to the fee accounts system described in Appendix E.

For smaller projects it may be feasible to describe the offer within the text of a letter, as shown in Figure D.8 on page 115. However, unless the job is very straightforward or the client is known to be fair minded, the description can become quite convoluted in the attempt to cover every eventuality.

Linked electronic systems are useful tools for compiling the offer and once the job has been won, but they can also be advantageous during face-to-face negotiations, if the offer requires adjustment.

Further information to support and enhance the submission might include:

- quality assurance status
- specialist skills available in-house
- details of recent commissions, including illustrations and contact names
- evidence of competency in health and safety issues, perhaps based on the RIBA Chartered Practice Health and Safety Policy Template
- types of building in which the practice has experience
- overseas experience and completed commissions, if relevant
- languages in which members of the practice are fluent, if relevant
- the team being offered for the particular commission, with brief CVs.

If the client has not confirmed the terms of the agreement to apply to the appointment, the offer should cover such matters as:

- terms and conditions, such as those found in the appropriate RIBA Agreement (see Section 7, page 57)
- roles of other consultants
- programme matters
- professional indemnity and other insurance cover offered.

The offer should always be made in writing. The covering letter should always be considered to be part of the presentation, even if the format of the offer is pre-determined by the client. The writing style must be crystal clear and concise, in language that the client will readily understand, and be persuasive. Avoid professional jargon and legalese. Keep testimonials and bland marketing puff separate from the prime issues. The text should show understanding of the client's requirements and the benefits of the approach (not just baldly stating how much it will cost). The objective is to engage, influence and persuade the client – to appoint you.

"The objective is to engage, influence and persuade"

Section 6
Negotiating the fee

In this Section:

- *Step 1: Developing negotiation skills*
- *Step 2: Analysing the issues*
- *Step 3: Bargaining and closure*

> *The key factors affecting clients' perceptions of value are not just the quality of advice but the delivery of understanding and explanation.*
>
> David Maister, *RIBA Journal*, October 2005

This section is primarily about negotiating the fee before an appointment is confirmed. However, the principles will be the same for negotiations at any time, which to be successful require development of the necessary skills, analysis of the issues and, finally, bargaining and closure.

When the right fee to do the job has been calculated and the offer has been made, the next step is to reach agreement with the client – that is where the architect's skills as a negotiator will come into play.

Step 1: Developing negotiation skills

Essentially, the architect negotiator will be selling professional services and the price, but as a contributor to RIBAnet said: 'We are not selling "drawings", we are selling knowledge, which either improves lifestyle, or property value or both' (5 March 2006).

At interview, a successful negotiator or team will:

- establish eye contact, smile or nod occasionally

- concentrate on what is being said
- be direct, but without arrogance
- be convincing and persuasive
- make points with assurance, but calmly, and then stop talking
- be commercially aware
- avoid personal bias or prejudice
- listen carefully and take notes.

Architects who find negotiations difficult should consider attending one of the many available seminars on salesmanship. Or just read the often very informative advertising blurb.

> *As I know from experience, fee negotiations and Greco-Roman wrestling are practically the same.*
>
> Chris Wise, *Building Magazine*, 14 August 2009

Step 2: Analysing the issues

Consider the objectives of the client, which may be to:

- clarify the offer
- understand the benefits of the offer
- reduce the fee or convert the fee to a fixed amount
- discover whether the relationship will prosper; a 'meeting of minds'.

Identify areas where compromise or changes to the structure of the offer may be possible or advantageous, for example:

- the calculated or variable lump sum fee option
- betterment or incentive fees
- improved programme.

Identify the potential for added value.

Most importantly, establish the base line at which negotiations will stop.

Step 3: Bargaining and closure

The architect who has completed steps 1 and 2 will start the negotiations with a clear strategy for the process. Negotiations are about each side moving towards each other's position – aim for a 'win–win' outcome.

*we wanted the jobs because they offered new architectural opportunities,
but I had to hide my enthusiasm and (implied) willingness to cut our fee.*
Simon Allford, *Architects' Journal*, 28 April 2005

In the negotiations:

- Seek out and recognise the client's values and objectives – are they the same as their needs?
- Aim high initially, move in small increments.
- Any offer must be conditional – 'If I do this, will you consider doing that?'
- Use questions to respond to a proposal.
- Nothing is agreed until everything is agreed, all issues are linked.
- Repeat points back to the other party, so that everyone is clear about the outcome.
- Always confirm what has been agreed or what further information is required, leaving no room for doubt later.

*Successful negotiation requires first, a systematic analysis of the problems
and issues involved and second, the interpersonal skills, ability to convince
and be convinced, and the ability to employ the bargaining ploys. There is
no successful negotiation without rigorous preparation.*
Robert White and Aleksandra Gregoric, *RIBA Journal*, March 2008

In fee negotiations, remember that the fee is the cost to the client of buying the architect's services and, from the client's point of view, would ideally be fixed. The risks to the architect of fixed fees lie in the degree of uncertainty in the project.

If reductions are proposed, the resource allocation method described in Appendix D could provide the information for the negotiations. The resource calculation sheets, perhaps with a separate list of the drawings required and the fee proposal, might be shared with the client to demonstrate the relationship between the services and the resources required for their delivery. (The actual resource costs should be confidential to the architect.)

Client and architect could consider together whether any of the tasks and/or resources could be eliminated. While the client may not wish to recognise the consequences of such reduction, it is vital that the architect is absolutely clear about the effect of any omissions on successful delivery of the project.

Of course, the architect might decide to carry some of the costs, e.g. certain expenses, or commercial pressures could mean that a choice must be made between not making a profit on a given project and downsizing the office with the loss of personnel.

If the negotiations are protracted, it may be necessary to consider whether the client is avoiding commitment, particularly if a request is made to start performing the services. While a contract requires 'offer and acceptance' to be complete, it may be reasonable to assume that a contract has come into force if, after receipt of an offer, the client's actions imply acceptance. If no response is received, it will be a matter for the architect's commercial judgement to decide whether to proceed with the services.

If the response is: 'Please get on with the services and we can negotiate', this will compromise the architect's position, particularly over the terms of any future contract and ownership of the copyright.

Treat such circumstances as working at risk, as discussed in Section 9.

Section 7
Getting paid and not getting paid

In this Section:

Getting paid
- *Golden rules for a healthy fee regime*
- *Provisions in the RIBA Agreements 2010 relating to fees*
- *Periodic payments*
- *The effect of market conditions*
- *Set-off*

Not getting paid
- *Recovering unpaid fees*
- *The options*
- *Debt recovery*

Getting paid

Golden rules for a healthy fee regime

- Always have a comprehensive agreement in writing.
- Make certain that the client understands the payment provisions.
- Use RIBA Agreements, wherever possible.
- Don't start any significant work until the agreement is signed.
- Carefully evaluate the cost of providing the services.
- Get the client to sign off and pay for:
  - the relevant work before initiating any activities with third parties, such as making applications to statutory or local authorities for planning or building regulations, or to freeholders or inviting tenders, and
  - each work stage as completed.

- Establish rigorous procedures for managing fee accounts, including routine credit-checking of clients.
- Keep a separate fee file, with copies of the agreement, all fee correspondence, file notes and submitted fee accounts. Keep it up to date at all times (see also page 119).
- Invoice monthly on every commission for any amount due, no matter how small.
- Submit claims for additional fees as incurred, not at the end of the commission – claiming additional fees on completion of the commission can surprise the client and lead to argument, late payment or, even worse, a counterclaim for some alleged negligence.

"only efficient management will ensure that payments are invoiced and received"

Payment will be a key feature of the agreement with the client, but only efficient management will ensure that payments are invoiced and received.

Provisions in the RIBA Agreements 2010 relating to fees

The RIBA Standard Agreement aims to provide fair and balanced terms in return for performance of the architect's services and includes an undertaking by the client to pay the amounts due to the architect.

The components of a Standard Agreement are the Conditions of Appointment, the Schedules, any appendices and a Memorandum of Agreement or Letter of Appointment.

The Schedules specify the project-specific details and include:

- the 'Project Data'
- 'The Services', which include a specification of the roles and services to be performed, and
- 'Fees and expenses'.

The Conditions of Appointment include:

- a definition of the Construction Cost
- definition of the selected fee option(s) – clauses 5.2–5.6

- provision for revision of lump sums and other rates – clause 5.7
- provision for adjustment of fees in the event of material change or if the architect incurs extra work or expense – clauses 5.8–5.11, and
- provision for payment on suspension or termination – clause 5.17–5.18.

The Conditions also include the following payment provisions:

5.14   *Payment under this Agreement shall be made as follows:*

5.14.1   *Payment shall become due to the Architect on the date of issue of the Architect's account. The final date for payment of any amount due to the Architect shall be 28 days from the issue of the relevant account.*

5.14.2   *The Architect shall issue accounts at intervals of not less than one month or as specified elsewhere in this Agreement setting out any accrued instalments of the fee and other amounts due, less any amounts previously paid and stating the basis of calculation of the amounts due. Instalments of fees shall be calculated on the Architect's reasonable estimate of the percentage of completion of the Services or stages or other services or any other specified method.*

5.14.3   *The Architect shall submit the final account for fees and any other amounts due when the Architect reasonably considers the Services have been completed.*

[A footnote to this clause says: 'In the event of non-payment of any amount properly due to the Architect under this Agreement, the Architect is entitled to interest on the unpaid amounts under the provisions of clause 5.19, may suspend use of the licence under the provisions of clause 6, may suspend or terminate performance of the Services and other obligations under the provisions of clause 8, or commence dispute resolution procedures and/or debt recovery procedures'.]

Payment notices

5.15   *The Client shall give a written notice to the Architect:*

5.15.1   *within 5 days of the date of issue of an account specifying the amount the Client proposes to pay and the basis of calculation of that amount; and*

5.15.2   *not later than 5 days before the final date for payment of any amount due to the Architect if the Client intends to withhold payment of any part of that amount stating the amount proposed to be withheld and the ground for doing so or, if there is more than one ground, each ground and the amount attributable to it.*

If no such notices are given the amount due shall be the amount stated as due in the account. The Client shall not delay payment of any undisputed part of the account.

Set-off

5.16   *The Client shall not withhold any amount due to the Architect under this agreement unless the amount has been agreed with the Architect or has been decided by any tribunal to which the matter is referred as not being due to the Architect.*

All rights of set-off at common law or in equity which the Client would otherwise be entitled to exercise are expressly excluded.

Late payment

5.19   *In the event that any amounts are not paid by the Client or the Architect when properly due, the payee shall be entitled to simple interest on such amounts until the date that payment is received at the daily rate equivalent to 8% over the dealing rate of the Bank of England Rate current at the date that payment becomes overdue, together with such costs reasonably incurred and duly mitigated by the payee (including costs of time spent by principals, employees and advisors) in obtaining payment of any sums due under this Agreement.*

The payee's entitlement to interest at the specified rate shall apply in respect of any amounts that are awarded in adjudication, arbitration or legal proceedings.

Recovery of costs

5.20   *The Client or the Architect shall pay to the other party who successfully pursues, resists or defends any claim or part of a claim brought by the other:*

5.20.1   *such costs reasonably incurred and duly mitigated (including costs of time spent by principals, employees and advisors) where the matter is resolved by negotiation or mediation; or*

5.20.2   *such costs as may be determined by any tribunal to which the matter is referred.*

Use of information

6.3.2   *if at any time the Client is in default of payment of any fees or other amounts properly due, the Architect may suspend further use of the licence on giving 7 days notice of the intention of doing so. Use of the licence may be resumed on receipt of such outstanding amounts; . . . .*

Suspension

8.1.2   *The Architect may suspend performance of the Services and/or other obligations on giving not less than 7 days' notice to the Client of the intention and stating the reasons for doing so in the event (a) that the Client fails to pay any fees or other amounts due by the final date for payment unless, where applicable, the Client has given effective notice under clause 5.15.2 of the intention to withhold payment of any part of an Architect's account; or . . . .*

These terms, with the possible exception of the no set-off provision, are compliant with the Housing Grants, Construction and Regeneration Act 1996 (HGCRA), which requires professional services contracts with business clients (but not domestic clients) to include the following provisions:

• the entitlement to stage payments or payment by instalments, except where the contract is, or is estimated to be, less than 45 days – but there is no prescription for the intervals and method of calculating the amounts due unless the Scheme for Construction Contracts applies
• the means of calculating the amount due and the date on which it is due, and the final date for payment
• payment may not be offset or withheld unless a notice has been given identifying the amount to be withheld and on what grounds – the notice cannot be issued after the final payment date (see also *Set-off*, page 65)
• the right to suspend performance of the contract on seven days' notice if the amount due has not been paid by the due date and no withholding notice has been issued
• payment cannot be made dependent on the receipt of money from a third party, except in the case of upstream insolvency, and
• the statutory right to refer disputes to adjudication.

The Concise Conditions of Appointment 2010

These Conditions are set out in concise terms and are broadly similar to the Standard Conditions.

The Conditions of Appointment for a Domestic Project 2010

Where the project is for work to the client's home, the domestic client will be:

- a 'consumer' to whom the Unfair Terms in Consumer Contracts Regulations 1999 (UTCCR) apply
- a 'residential occupier' exempt from the provisions of the HGCRA, and
- exempt from the Late Payment of Commercial Debts (Interest) Regulations 2002.

The UTCCR require that the terms of any agreement, including the fee, must always be negotiated with a 'consumer' client. Of particular concern would be any clauses which 'inappropriately exclude or limit the legal rights of the consumer'; for that reason, there is no provision to exclude the rights to set-off or joint and several liability, as in a net contribution clause.

In other respects the Conditions are based on the same principles as the Standard Agreement. Note, however, that the payment period is 14 days.

The Conditions for Appointment for a Sub-Consultant 2010

If sub-consultants are to be retained to perform part of the architect's services, ensure that:

- they have agreed to be appointed and named their fee prior to making a fee offer to the client
- the agreement will be compatible with the head agreement with the client, and
- they are willing to warrant performance to the client.

The Conditions in the Sub-Consultant Agreement include broadly similar provisions relating to payment and non-payment to the Standard Agreement. Note, however, that the payment period is 42 days.

Periodic payments

There are several options for periodic payments:

- monthly, based on the architect's estimated percentage of completion – the default provision in RIBA Agreements
- at completion of a work stage or other milestone
- by equalised instalments.

Whichever option is chosen, there is less risk from unexpected change where separate fees for each work stage or group of stages are agreed. Once a stage has been completed and paid for there can be no change or re-examination of the amount. It may also be that the limitation period will run from the date of the invoice for the completed stage (see Alistair McGrigor, 'The final analysis', *RIBA Journal*, January 2006).

Staged payments will also protect front-loaded fees in the event that the appointment or the project is cancelled or changed significantly. Where percentage fees apply, in the pre-construction period monthly invoices could be calculated on the latest approved cost. During the construction period a percentage fee might be similarly treated or based on the certified value each month unless the time charge option is adopted.

Alternatively, the fee can be divided into equal instalments for each month in the programme where the duration of each stage or group of stages is more than two or three months and completion of the project is reasonably ensured.

Even so, it is recommended that fees are work stage based to avoid the difficulties of unexpected change. The calculations would be revisited if there were changes to the programme and/or the cost. This option does not apply where the option of time charges for the construction stages (RIBA Work Stages H to L1) is preferred.

The author knows at least one architect who arranges for prearranged instalments to be paid by direct debit!

The agreed arrangement might be set down in a fee management plan, which is used to calculate periodic payments and cash flows and to show the effect on the fee of changes in the relevant cost or to the programme (see Figure E.2, page 121). Where the project, or just the building contract, is to be completed in sections, it may be appropriate to divide the total fee in proportion to the cost of construction of each section for each work stage.

In *Getting Paid* by Nicholas J. Carnell and Steven Yakeley (RIBA Enterprises, 2003) the suggestion is made that the agreement should require all fees for RIBA Work Stages C to K to be paid before the architect issues the Certificate of Practical Completion, leaving only Work Stage L1 to follow. It is noted that, as funders or mortgagors often require a completion certificate before making the final payment, clients may be less inclined to quibble about the fees.

Further, the wise architect should formulate and submit any claim for any additional fees prior to this point.

Leslie Wise notes (see page 71) that a few bold architects stipulate that they must be paid half their fees (half of each work stage) in advance.

The effect of market conditions

Inflation

In times of inflation, increases in the cost of building and running the practice are covered in RIBA Conditions by linking percentage or calculated lump sum fees to the Construction Cost and/or the provisions for revision of lump sums, time charges and other rates. Obviously, the architect will need to consider whether such increases apply if the increase is not due to market conditions!

Deflation

Predetermined fees – percentages or lump sums – are based on the assumption that the fee will cover the cost of providing the Services.

But in times of deflation, interim estimates or tender prices may be lower than predicted, although the input required does not change. Only time charges escape this trap.

To cover this situation, RIBA Standard Conditions provide at clause 5.8.2:

> *[The Basic Fee] shall not be adjusted for any reduction of the Construction Cost arising solely from deflationary market conditions not prevailing at the Effective Date. The Basic Fee shall continue to be based on the Construction Cost current prior to the date of such reduction.*

Otherwise, a fee based on a single percentage would be particularly vulnerable as instalments already paid could be adjusted retrospectively.

Another consequence in a recession may be a rise in bad debts or late payments. Routine checking of clients' credit ratings may give an early warning of trouble ahead. Many banks now offer a credit-checking service to small businesses. The Department for Business, Innovation and Skills has produced a series of Managing Cashflow Guides, available at: www.creditmanagement.org.uk/berrguides.htm.

Set-off

The common law right of set-off provides a remedy where one party can rely on a separate claim to reduce or extinguish liability to the other.

It is a regrettable fact that clients make claims of negligence, often spurious or just because of some disappointment, and use this right of set-off as a device for avoiding payment of fees properly due, often in the closing stages of the commission.

Because this is not an uncommon factor in an architect's life, the RIBA decided, after much debate, to continue to exclude the right of set-off in RIBA Conditions of Appointment (clause 5.16) (but not in the conditions for a domestic project), with the intention of:

• separating payment of fees (cash flow) from damages, if the alleged negligence is proven, payable under the architect's indemnity insurance policy, and encouraging the client to make a realistic assessment of success before pursuing any claim at adjudication or in court.

The counter argument

In the long debate and in the press, concern was expressed by lawyers and others about the uncertain relationship of the no set-off provision in clause 5.16 with clause 5.15.

Clause 5.15 gives effect to the requirement of the HGCRA that 'a party to a construction contract may not withhold payment... unless he has given an effective notice of intention to withhold payment'. Under this clause, the client's right of abatement is not affected if the no set-off provision is deleted.

Rachel Barnes (*Building*, 10 July 2009) wrote:

> *it may still be possible for potentially spurious claims to comply with the requirements of the notice. However, realistically there is nothing that can be done about that except to challenge the notice. If the purpose of a no set-off clause is in fact to exclude all rights of set-off in a construction contract, even of amounts that have been the subject of a valid withholding notice, this would not be consistent with the intention of the act. The main purpose of the withholding notice is to protect the payee, by making the payer give proper details of the amount that it intends to withhold.*

> *However, it follows that the payer also has a right to give such a notice and then to withhold the amount in question. That right is conferred by the act, and any attempt to take it away would be ineffective.*

The legal process may not be as simple as the no set-off clause intends.

There is a risk that if a claim is referred to the courts, it might be decided that the clause is unfair under the Unfair Contract Terms Act 1977. In the case of a consumer client, it would almost certainly not survive the impact of the UTCCR.

There is also established authority that the courts wish litigants to bring all their related claims at the same time rather than to risk successive, costly items of litigation. Should, therefore, an architect pursue a client for recovery of fees the court may reject an application to exclude any counterclaim on the basis that no right of set-off exists.

Not getting paid

> *You are more likely to become involved in a legal dispute over your fees than any other issue in your practice.*
>
> Owen Luder

Anything which disrupts cash flow can be stressful, or worse. However, even the most meticulous management of finances cannot ensure all accounts will be paid on time.

If the client does not pay it might be due to accidental oversight, to a systematic policy of late payment, or to deliberate non-payment by set-off for a claim against the architect.

Recovering unpaid fees

The first step, perhaps in a telephone call, is to discover the reasons for the non-payment and/or to obtain a firm date for payment. If necessary this could be followed by a letter drawing attention to the terms of the contract, as in the footnote to the payment clause (see page 59).

If there is any indication that the client is in financial difficulty, the architect will need to consider whether to strike a deal, i.e. settle for less, recognising that if the client becomes insolvent, the architect as a potentially unsecured creditor might not recover any of the costs, let alone the fees.

If it is clear that the client believes they have a genuine complaint, the next step is to determine whether a negotiated settlement could be achieved.

If this is not possible, send a further letter to the client drawing attention to the no set-off clause and demanding payment. The letter should also suggest that the client uses the dispute resolution procedures to settle the matter, and that the architect is referring the matter to the insurers.

If the architect's insurers have not already been notified of the potential dispute, now is the time do so.

If the allegation of default was made just to avoid payment, the client may choose to repent rather than face any formal dispute resolution tribunal.

In addition, as an alternative or where the client is a consumer, the architect can exercise the contractual options:

- to claim interest on the unpaid amounts, and/or
- to suspend use of the copyright licence, and/or
- to suspend or terminate performance of the Services, and/ or
- to commence dispute resolution procedures, or
- to commence debt recovery procedures (see page 71).

This scenario would apply whether or not the client issued a withholding notice or, for that matter, whether the set-off clause was deleted.

It would also provide the most appropriate options where the client ignores the contractual provisions and just hangs on to the money but the archi-tect is reluctant to instigate proceedings against the client, as in most cases an architect's PI policy will not cover the legal costs arising.

> *See also:*
> *Recovery of*
> *costs, page 70*

However, before exercising any of the options, the architect should consider the possible reaction of the client, whether the situation can be remedied in any other way and how any potential loss can be minimised, and if necessary seek legal advice. Late payment in itself does not justify termination, but if it is a regular practice of the client, termination on giving *reasonable* notice might be appropriate.

The options

Interest on late payments

In the event of non-payment of an account, RIBA Agreements include a provision for *both business and domestic clients* to claim simple interest at 8 per cent over base rate and to recover the reasonable costs of obtaining payment. Note that the clause applies to a valid debt of the architect to the client, such as an award to the client by an adjudicator.

Where the client enters a contract in the course of business, an alternative to this contractual arrangement is to specify in the agreement that the statutory provisions of the Late Payment of Commercial Debts (Interest) Regulations 2002 will apply.

Where the regulations apply, interest is chargeable at 8 per cent over the base interest rate. The rate in force on 30 June applies for the period 1 July to 31 December. Then the base rate on 31 December will apply to the next six months, and so on.

The Better Payment Practice Group (www.payontime.co.uk) publishes the *The Late Payment of Commercial Debts (Interest) Act 1998: A user's guide*, which provides useful information about the operation of the regulations and an interest calculator. The section on 'Excuses' includes guidance on credit management and the risks and provides specimen letters and forms. Although the regulations only apply to transactions between businesses, the clause also applies to domestic clients.

Copyright licence

The option of suspending this licence to use the drawings or similar materials on giving seven days' notice is a powerful tool. The drawings etc. may be used by contractors, local authorities, funders, mortgagors, facility managers or other parties. Therefore, the notice could draw to the attention of the client that continued use by any such 'other persons' will also be a breach of copyright, and that the suspension will continue until receipt of the outstanding amounts.

Suspension of performance of the Services

Performance of the Services and other obligations under the agreement can be suspended, after giving at least seven days' notice, in the event of non-payment by all clients, provided in the case of a business client that no withholding notice has been given. A condition in the Domestic Project Conditions provides a variant of the withholding notice, but there is no statutory requirement for this.

This may be an effective remedy while the pre-construction, construction or post-completion stages are in progress. As noted previously, the completion certificate is often needed by clients for their funders or mortgagors. This option may be less effective if it is the final payment that is withheld, in which case the alternatives will lie in the agreed dispute resolution procedures or debt collection.

Litigation

If the client has indicated in writing the intention to pay but repeated reminders have had no effect, one option is to pursue the matter in court. Referral to the courts would also be appropriate if the dispute relates to the enforcement of the decision of an adjudicator. Claims for less than £5,000 can be pursued using the small claims procedure in the county courts.

Adjudication

If the client has not responded to any request for payment, then adjudication may be an option. RIBA Forms of Appointment require the issue by the client of a notice of the intention to withhold payment of any part of an account; in the case of a business client this is a statutory requirement under the HGCRA.

If the client has failed to issue any notice or notices this would mean that there would be little that the client could raise by way of defence. In addition, an adjudication notice by the architect requiring payment of the invoices would define the dispute, therefore the client would not be able to raise any counter-claim regarding negligence. The claim may therefore stand a good chance of succeeding.

Negligence claims

However, if the client has made a claim alleging lack of performance, negligence or some similar matter, before selecting adjudication it may be appropriate to consider whether the particular allegation of negligence is suitable for adjudication.

If the client has raised complex arguments in support of the refusal to pay, then the best solution may be litigation or arbitration (depending on which has been selected in the agreement). In deciding the strategy for defending the claim, the architect (or the insurers) will need to consider whether to rely on the no set-off provision in the RIBA Standard and Concise Conditions.

Recovery of costs

RIBA Agreements provide for the reasonable costs of a successful claimant to be paid by the other party in respect of a valid debt or for other claims where the matter is resolved by negotiation or mediation.

It should be noted that in most cases an architect's PI policy will not cover the architect's costs of obtaining payment. If negotiations do not achieve a result, debt recovery procedures may provide a solution.

However, if the matter cannot be resolved and is referred to adjudication, arbitration or the courts, the costs recoverable by the winning party will be limited to the costs determined by the tribunal (the maximum payable under a losing architect's PI policy).

Other options

Other options for resolution of the problem of non-payment are discussed in:

- *The Handbook* – Claiming Fees, Section 13
- *Getting Paid* by Nicholas J. Carnell and Steven Yakeley (RIBA Enterprises, 2003), which gives useful guidance on the process once a formal dispute has arisen
- *The Architect's Guide to Running a Practice* by David Littlefield (Architectural Press, 2005), which includes a performance standard for debt collection drawn up by Sobell Rhodes Chartered Accountants, and
- the articles on debt recovery by Leslie Wise reproduced on pages 71–75.

Debt recovery *by Leslie Wise*

RIBA Journal, April and May 2005

'Collect call'

The law on collection of money from clients is now much more user-friendly. If you have tried everything else it is now much easier to get on and sue as a result of Lord Justice Woolf's Civil Procedure Reforms. The courts have responded by improving the follow-up measures.

But before this stage is reached, you need to explore all basic means of solving the problem of outstanding debt. A few bold architects have already helped reduce the problem by stipulating that they must be paid half their fees (half of each work stage) in advance. Submitting invoices promptly helps cash flow and it is not unusual to expect payment within 14 days (I sometimes get seven days if subject to some sort of discount). As one architect I spoke to recently put it, either the clients have the money or they haven't.

When payment is late the first step should be a telephone call to the client. Some people find that difficult, but sending in a second account is not much good. I am head of a debt collection agency and in my experience a written reminder rarely works. Our first letter is polite, pithy – and ignored. Try a telephone call and be sure to speak directly to the non-paying party. Don't be put off and remember that a call can sometimes ensure that you jump the queue and get paid ahead of others.

If the client pleads financial difficulties suggest, as an alternative to suing, that payments are made in instalments, preferably by post-dated cheques at regular intervals or perhaps by credit card. Once you have the client's undertakings to pay off the debt regularly, you have much more important things to do than chase payments. So if the debtor promises a payment by a certain date, put it in your diary and have someone contact them before the cheque is due. Or, as soon as the first post has arrived without payment. Persistence will help avoid the need to go to court.

If the debt is for more than £750, a further and serious last step often worth considering is the sending in of a *Statutory Demand*. There is a simple form to fill in (downloadable from the web at www.insolvency.gov.uk/pdfs/forms/6-1.pdf) and it needs to come to the attention of the actual debtor, so strictly speaking it needs to be hand delivered. You can still send the form by post, in which case it will be more as a bluff rather than the intention of action. To be most effective the form is best delivered by a process server (you can find one in the *Yellow Pages* and they usually cost in the region of £80 to £100). That way the debtor is confronted – always a nasty shock – and the server will swear proof that the necessary formalities have been complied with. The process server's report often describes the person he served.

The demand gives a debtor two alternatives: pay within 18 days (or a compromise to your reasonable satisfaction); or risk you applying to the courts for a bankruptcy/winding up order depending on whether the debtor is an individual or a company.

If you are using the latter route, the trick is not to limit yourself to sending the demand to the usual recipients. Ensue that senior officers and all the directors know about it too. There are protocols and a few pitfalls (chief of which is that the courts refuse to act as enforcers and may penalise unsuccessful applicants in costs if they are considered to have acted oppressively, but a demand properly used invariably stirs things up and almost always produces results.

If all else has failed, sue. Before following this path, it is worth warning the debtor that you intend to sue and are in the process of taking this action. There is no legal protocol requiring you to issue this warning, but the delay is slight and this final indication of intent sometimes produces the desired result. There is no need to spell out the costs, but this also can be desirable. They are small enough, but the debtor may not know that. It should help to point out that those costs of the action will be for the debtor to pay.

'Courtly actions'

There is a raft of methods for getting overdue debts paid but, when all else fails, suing the debtor may be the only choice.

Since July 2002 creditors have been entitled to charge interest on late payments at the swingeing rate of 8 per cent over base rate, so if you are suing there is no reason for not suing for the maximum. It is worth including a claim for interest following judgment too. The courts also seem to accept an administration charge of £40 as reasonable.

The one reason not to sue for the maximum is to keep your court costs down. If you win, the debtor will pay the costs, but if the debtor proves later to be insolvent you will have been throwing a bit less good money after bad. Court fees are based on the size of the sum you are claiming (from £30 if the sum exceeds £300 to £250 for sums exceeding £5,000 but not £15,000). So if your total claim is near an upper limit, for example £5,050, It might be prudent to sue for £5,000 and restrict court costs to £120.

Some creditors prefer to use a solicitor, who will quote a fixed price. However, since the Woolf Civil Procedure Reforms it is easy to do it yourself. All you need is a claim form, which is obtainable from the local county court or the Internet and is simple to complete. Alternatively, you can sue online (for up to £100,000). Go to www.moneyclaim.gov.uk, and follow the steps. The costs are the same whether you sue online or off, they are payable by credit card and your writ could be issued by 10 a.m. the next day.

If the defendant does not enter a defence within 18 days you can claim Judgment in Default by using the court form or online. The clock starts ticking from the hypothetical date of service, not the date of issue. You can't rely on the court to follow your claim through, after the elapsed time you may have to nag. I usually just send a fax to the Clerk of the Court. They have never replied to me but the cause of complaint is actioned almost immediately thereafter. If you have sued online then a dally visit to the claim will tell you when you may request judgment.

Once granted, you have an order of the court and if you want you can be quite open about collecting the money without fear of falling foul of the law under the Administration of Justice Act 1972. The words 'debt collection' in red on correspondence attracts attention and, following judgment, is perfectly acceptable.

But before resorting to your weapons of enforcement and the associated expense, consider again whether the debtor is worth powder and shot. You can do this by filing a request for information (formerly an oral examination). This is a method of asking the court to interrogate the debtor. For £40 it will summon the debtor to complete a questionnaire requiring details of bank accounts, landlords, other creditors, other debtors, assets sold, cars owned and any current contracts – including their details and value, any expected stage payments, when, how much and so on. If you want you can attend the interrogation and may put in your pennyworth too (but be sure to tell the clerk you are there). If the creditor fails to attend on a second occasion it may be contemptuous and carry a prison sentence.

Thus, hopefully properly informed, you can decide how you will try to extract the money. There are a series of remedies to choose from: earnings attachment order; third party debt order; a charging order; sending in the bailiffs; or just writing the debt off. What does each involve?

Bailiffs

Using court bailiffs, which are officers of the court and paid by the court, is the remedy most often adopted. However, more than half the orders are returned unsatisfied because, disgracefully, the creditor has not given the bailiff the correct name or the address of the debtor.

Third party debt order

This is the new name for 'a garnishee order' – which no one understood. It is an order from the court to your judgment debtor's debtor (someone who owes your debtor money) to pay that money directly to you. The order is made on application and, for obvious reasons, is most commonly used against banks. However, there is no reason why it can't be used against your debtors' customers.

Attachment of earnings orders

These are only used for smaller debts and are *vastly unpopular*. A proportion of earnings from employees is used to pay the debt. Employers also have a duty to disclose, if they know it, the address of the debtor's next job when they move. Research shows that the debtor does just that – perhaps to avoid the order or, as anecdotal evidence suggests, the move may be originated by the employer. Their unpopularity is perhaps a reason the charging order survives as a useful tool.

Charging order

If the debtor has property there is a simple form requesting that a charge be registered against it. This charge is really just a means of ensuring that your debt is secured, because no court is likely to order the sale of a property unless the debt is substantial. The days are gone when an architect had to sigh and write a debt off. The courts are there to help the small creditor too. It is worth availing yourself of these rights more often.

Section 8
Fee adjustments, managing change

In this Section:

- *Change control*
- *Changes to the architect's work*
- *Changes and the basic fee*
- *Calculating fee adjustments*

After appointment, as the fee or fees may need to be adjusted for any number of reasons, the provisions of the agreement with the client for fee adjustment will be particularly important.

Forms of appointment, such as those published by the RIBA, will provide for remunerating any architect involved in extra work or expense or liability for reasons not envisaged at the beginning and perhaps for various rates or lump sums to be adjusted for inflation. Beware in bespoke contracts of any provisions which are described in ambiguous terms or which limit payment strictly to additional services arising from a client's instruction (although the wise architect always notifies the client on becoming aware that additional services will be required).

"Provisions for fee adjustment will be particularly important"

Change control

A procedure to record changes to the services or completed design information will provide a proper basis for claims for additional or adjusted fees. For small projects, this might be achieved in conjunction with the time records (see Figure C.1, page 96).

For larger projects it may be appropriate to establish a procedure for change control requiring all proposed changes affecting other parties to be notified, approved and recorded, together with the cost consequences, including fees, the initiator, the date and a reference number.

Changes to the architect's work

The iterative design process will always generate changes to the architect's work, which will have a cost to the architect, but may not generate an entitlement to additional fees unless the changes are instructed by the client or the performance of the services is delayed, disrupted or prolonged.

But there are unlikely to be provisions in the agreement for additional fees for changes arising from design development or from integration of the work of others, etc. Obviously, the architect must bear the cost of revising the design if it does not comply with the brief – for instance, if the cost of constructing the design will exceed any cost limit.

As noted in Section 3 (page 26), RIBA Work Stage F (Production Information) may be carried out in two parts. As the division between the two parts cannot be predicted, no provision can be made to split the fee for Work Stage F, but resources may have to be reserved until Work Stages J, K and L1.

Changes and the basic fee

See also: The effect of market conditions, page 64

Whenever changes occur, for whatever reason, the basic fee, whether percentage based or lump sum, may also be affected, as detailed below.

Percentage fees

Fees based on a percentage of the final cost of construction will be adjusted automatically. The movement would be down if the cost goes down but up if the cost goes up; provided, of course, that any increase in cost does not exceed any limit on expenditure. The definition of the cost of construction will be important in relation to any contingency sum, loss and/or expense payments and liquidated damages.

Lump sums

Where fees are based on calculated lump sums, the situation will be similar to percentage fees in the pre-construction stages. However, in the construction stages, Work Stages J and K, the relevant lump sums will be fixed by the accepted tender price, including any contingency sum, and no further adjustments can be made unless the agreement allows for adjustment, for example for additional services. Where fixed lump sum fees apply, no other fees are payable unless the agreement allows for such adjustment.

Time charges

Where the fee for performance of the services is based on time charges, the records will be important, particularly if a budget for the time-based fees has been agreed. If these records are to be used to justify additional fees, they should be sufficiently explicit to identify the extra work. Phrases such as 'altering drawings' or 'drawing work' or 'attending meeting' may prove to be woefully inadequate in a formal dispute tribunal.

If the fees for Work Stages J, K and L1 are charged on a time basis, such fees must be rigorously accounted for. Time spent in the preparation of further production information must be excluded if the basic fee includes for Work Stage F2.

Calculating fee adjustments

The following examples explain when adjustments might be made to the basic fee, i.e. for 'normal' services and when additional fees (called 'other fees' in RIBA Forms) might become due. It will be apparent that, regardless of the fee basis, it is preferable to specify separately for each work stage the relevant percentage, lump sum or any budget for time charges.

Revision to brief or client's instructions

As an example, if the client decides to move the accounts department to another building and replace it with a design studio, additional fees would be due on a time basis or, if appropriate, an agreed lump sum until the revised requirements are incorporated into the design, after which the basic fee arrangement will apply, based on the updated cost of construction. In the case of fixed lump sums, there may be a case to argue that the subsequent lump sums should be adjusted, if the agreement allows for such adjustment.

Acceleration

If the client decides to modify the timetable to achieve earlier occupation, budgets, time charges or fixed lump sums might be agreed for each work stage affected. The budgets or lump sums should be based on a best estimate, taking into account the facts that:

- additional resources may be required, perhaps including overtime working
- some works might be covered by provisional measurement or sums requiring design information to be prepared or modified during the construction period
- the contract administration period would be reduced, although the volume of construction work would remain the same
- it may not be possible to foresee all the risks.

The biggest difficulty may be to agree or determine the starting point from which the additional resources would be chargeable.

Omission of work in the original brief or cost of construction

The initial fee calculation will be based on the whole project and, inevitably, some parts of the services will be subsidised by other parts requiring fewer resources. Omission of a substantial element could upset the balance of the fee; for instance, it might be decided at the end of RIBA Work Stage D that the production equipment, previously included in the cost of construction, should be a direct contract without the involvement of the architect.

Where either the percentage fee or the calculated lump sums method applies, the basic fee would be adjusted downwards although the architect had provided the necessary services. If the cost of construction had been £2.5 million, of which the equipment installation was £0.5 million and a 6 per cent overall fee applied, the architect might claim:

- 6 per cent × 40 per cent (at Work Stage D) × £0.5 million, plus
- time charges for removing references from the design information.

(If fixed lump sum or sums apply, a similar, but more difficult, calculation would be necessary.)

Client variations during the construction period

Where the client requires changes to be made during the construction period, the provisions of the agreement for extra work will apply. Note that where the basic fee is calculated as a percentage fee and the inclusion of the variations reduces the cost of construction, the basic fee will be reduced also. However, if the variations increase the cost of construction, in addition to any other fees claimable, the basic fee covering the design and construction stages will also increase.

Research into additional facilities

If the architect is asked to investigate the provision of an additional facility, for instance an additional floor, the research and report will be chargeable under the provisions of the agreement for extra work, whether or not the facility is included in the project. If included, the basic fee would be adjusted for the next work stages, as noted under 'Revision to brief or client's instructions' above.

Section 9
Working at risk, working for something

In this Section:

- *Preliminary services*
- *Speculative or conditional offers*

Preliminary services

Architects may be invited to provide preliminary services – usually design services, perhaps in competition with others, and with or without a fee proposal.

If the client is the future owner of the building, the objective may be to obtain:

- planning permission, or
- approval in principle by a funder.

If the client is a contractor, the objective may be to obtain:

- a design and build or development contract, or
- 'preferred bidder' status in PFI/PPP-type projects. (Note, in public sector work the subsequent appointment of the architect might be subject to EC requirements for competition.)

An architect may also enter an open architectural competition.

Before proceeding, architects must decide on their practice strategy and, in each case, make a commercial judgement about the risks involved.

Speculative or conditional offers

Of course, until an agreement is reached with the client any response is 'speculative' and it is inherent in a speculative offer that the architect is, in effect, saying:

'I will wager achievement of your objective against some (or all) of my preliminary fee'.

It is important, therefore, to know or record the terms on which the offer is made. Working 'at risk' should not be an option; there is always danger when the optimistic courts the unscrupulous. The law does not generally support claims for payment for doing work in the expectation of obtaining a contract. The bidding process is speculative and the associated costs are not normally recoverable.

Nevertheless, an architect providing preliminary services at the request of a client, whether building owner, developer or contractor, might in certain circumstances make a successful claim on a *quantum meruit*. In the absence of a contract, a claim would be based on the principle that the law will require the client to make restitution if the client has not paid for the architect's work which helped to achieve the client's objectives and/or the anticipated subsequent contract was not awarded to the architect.

For a claim to succeed it would be necessary to demonstrate that the architect's contribution was:

- requested by the client and given on the mutual understanding that a contract would follow
- of benefit to the client.

Of course, it is implicit in speculative offers that there is no guarantee that the architect's input will be rewarded at the end of the day, unless the offer specifies that payment of fees and expenses is due whatever the outcome. This may be of no great consequence if it amounts to a few sketches and the odd meeting, but there must be a defined cut-off point for such 'free' work.

Wherever there is risk, if for no other reason, the offer should be given a job number and records kept of the time spent. It will then be possible to assess the cost of the job and, if it proceeds, even to recover the cost of some of the preliminary work and, if not, provide valuable information for the next speculation.

The *ARB Architect's Code of Conduct and Practice* requires an architect to define the terms of engagement before services are provided (Standard 11) and 'at all times to act with integrity' (Standard 1). Compliance with these requirements will uphold professional standards and safe practice in a world of commercial predators. If, contrary to the Code, the architect simply does whatever is required and hopes for the best, the risk to the architect's reward will be at its highest.

An offer (such as the speculative offer specimen letter shown on pages 86–88) will provide the basis for a contract and should therefore:

- be as carefully considered as any other bid
- be addressed to the potential client, state what the offer comprises, the conditions that would apply on acceptance of the offer and to any subsequent appointment, and the liability for fees arising, and
- attempt to protect the copyright in any work produced by and prevent exploitation of the architect by the client, whether building owner or contractor.

While a contract requires 'offer and acceptance' to be complete, it may be reasonable to assume that a contract has come into force if, after receipt of an offer, the client's actions imply acceptance. If no response is received, it will be another matter for the architect's commercial judgement on whether to proceed with the services. If the response is: 'Please get on with the services and we can negotiate', the effect may be to confuse the architect's position, particularly over the terms of any future contract and ownership of the copyright.

Speculative offer specimen letter to a contractor client

IVOR B'ARCH Architects LLP

Prospect Drive Thawbridge BS17 2ZX

T: 0100 012 023
F: 0100 012 024
E: ivor@b'arch.com

RIBA ₩
Chartered Practice

Contractors Ltd   22 February 20XX

Barset Park

Barset

BS17 6YZ   Our ref: 423/IB/0112

For the attention of Mr James Smith

Dear Sir

Proposed Retail Park Barset

We write to confirm that you have asked us to join your team preparing a tender submission for this design and build project and to confirm the terms of our appointment.

You have provided an outline of your requirements and a copy of the tender documents and asked us to:

1 carry out some feasibility studies for the project: in particular to identify solutions (a) suitable for a development adjoining the conservation area, and (b) which will minimise energy usage; and subsequently;

2 to develop the preferred solution sufficient for the purposes of the tender submission.

For the above services to be provided effectively, you have agreed we shall act as lead designer and you will obtain structural and building services designs and cost advice to assist us. We understand that a measured survey of the site, the existing services and the ground conditions [is available] [will be made available].

Performance of our services will be carried out [for a lump sum fee of £ ___] [on a time-charged basis]. If other preliminary services are required these will be charged additionally on a time basis. Time-based services are charged at the following rates:

Principal: £ ___ per hour   Senior architect: £ ___ per hour

These preliminary charges include out-of-pocket expenses but exclude special presentation material and any disbursements made on your behalf. An account will be submitted on completion of our preliminary services. VAT [is] [is not] chargeable on the net value of our fees and expenses.

We will perform the preliminary services in accordance with the RIBA Standard Conditions for the Appointment of an Architect, with supplementary agreement Contractor's Design Services, copies of which are enclosed, subject to the following:

- 50 per cent of our fees will become payable on the date set for the tender submission;
- the remaining 50 per cent will become payable on acceptance by the building owner of the submission;
- additional fees shall be paid for any services provided after submission and prior to further appointment;
- fees shall be due whether or not the project proceeds;
- if we are not appointed to perform further services, a premium payment of £X, incorporating the licence fee for the copy and use of our design, shall become payable, whether or not the design is adopted as the basis for the project.

It is a condition of this offer that RIBA Standard Conditions of Contract and the supplementary agreement Contractor's Design Services are also the basis for the further services required (Work Stages J, D, E, F, K and L) to complete the project, for which our further fees will amount in total to ___ per cent of the cost of construction, including provision for your overheads and profit.

Additionally, out-of-pocket expenses, including printing, reproduction and travelling costs, will be charged by the addition of ___ per cent to the gross fees payable [at net cost plus ___ per cent handling charge]. Special presentation material and any disbursements made on your behalf will be charged at net cost plus ___ per cent.

If these terms are acceptable, please sign the enclosed copy of this letter and return it to us. We shall then be in a position to start work. We are looking forward to working with you on this project.

Yours faithfully

Ivor B'Arch

for and on behalf of Ivor B'Arch Architects LLP

_____

I/We confirm that Ivor B'Arch Architects LLP is to proceed with the preliminary services as set out above.

[signed] *James Smith* for *Contractors Ltd* [date] *20th March 20XX*

Appendix A
Simple management systems

The management toolbox

The practice management toolbox will need to include manual or electronic systems for:

- recording time usage and calculating the cost of that time
- day-to-day accounting or book-keeping
- resource planning and resource monitoring
- calculating fee offers and invoicing clients, and
- identifying the practice's workload over time and monitoring progress.

These systems should be compatible with, or part of, the quality assurance procedures adopted by the practice or the *RIBA Quality Management Toolkit*.

Each system should provide the information required by the others (see Figure A.1). There are obvious benefits if information covering all practice expenditure is available to give a picture of the practice's financial health.

Whichever systems are used, the files should be saved in a library of historical data, which can be used to improve the accuracy of future predictions and charges.

For demonstration purposes, linked spreadsheets (such as Microsoft Excel) are used to create the component parts of a system.

If it is necessary to identify every fee-earning time unit (usually 15 minutes), the records should also include time spent on telephone calls, e-mails, etc. The issue of relevance to related time-charged fees must be taken into account, particularly if the fees may be subject to audit by the client.

This can be achieved using database systems such as Microsoft Access, or Microsoft Outlook with Estos Pro software (www.estos.com) to create an Outlook Journal logging telephone calls or e-mails, in or out, time spent performing routine technical tasks and saving all Excel and Word files by job number. The journal can be searched to sort the data by job number as a preparatory step to preparing invoices.

Of course, such refinements can be ignored, but the data would have to be sorted manually by project, date and activity at the end of each month to produce the necessary information for the preparation of invoices. The more projects there are, the longer it will take. The time spent in the analysis and the loss of accurate time records has the effect of increasing overheads.

Alternatively, a commercial electronic package, which provides each system separately or in combination, could be purchased. The chosen system should be compatible for easy integration of the data with any accounting package in use. A list of some of the commercial time and cost management systems for architects is given as Table A.1. Some packages work in conjunction with or include accounting software and forecast fee income and record fees invoiced and received.

For simplicity, in this guide the worked examples are based on linked spreadsheets for a small practice with a sole principal, two professionals, one technologist and a secretary/office manager.

Book-keeping

In the context of fee management and the practice's financial health, it will be necessary to maintain accurate records of day-to-day transactions, such as a cash book, a list of unpaid bills and a list of unpaid fee invoices. In addition, a separate record of all payments to any employed staff should be maintained, together with tax deducted, PAYE, National Insurance, etc.

Book-keeping records can be maintained manually or using one of the commercially available book-keeping and accounting software packages. The records should be studied and analysed; they will often reveal where waste is occurring or economies can be made, or where stricter control is needed.

A Guide to Managing IT (RIBA Publications, 2001) recommends that, when choosing software to deal with book-keeping, its functionality should be considered in terms of practice needs:

- Is financial information to be exchanged electronically with the practice's accountant?
- How will moving existing financial information to the new system be dealt with? One of the biggest headaches when it comes to accounting can be attempting to migrate from one system to another. Different systems store information in different ways and trying to make the conversion from one to another can be frustratingly difficult. The manufacturers of the new system will probably be able to help, but it makes sense to run both side by side for a time until things settle down.
- Does the new software integrate with the time management system?
- Does the software allow for downloading information directly from the practice bank's online service to save keying in all of the information? Even if online banking is not used now, it may be in the future.
- Does the software provide facilities to try out 'what if' scenarios?

Accounting packages have to be generic business tools, so they include facilities for many different types of business, including sales and manufacturing. Try to find a package that 'understands' the service industries.

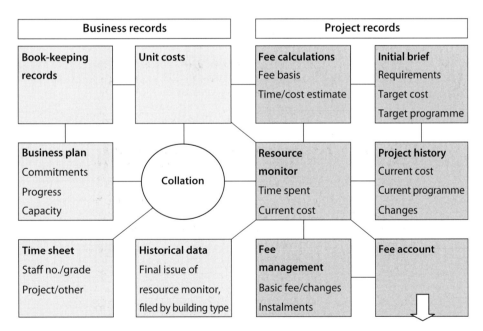

FIGURE A.1: *Relationship of system files*

Workload

Software programmes are available that provide Gantt charts to give a graphic overview of what is happening in the office and/or on particular projects. Such software makes producing this kind of chart very easy, and is particularly good for:

- planning what people are going to be doing in the future, and for how long
- monitoring progress against projections
- editing the information or trying out alternative scenarios
- changing the length of time a task is expected to take or moving the start date
- changing the start date of one task and automatically changing linked tasks correspondingly
- tracking actual progress against the initial plan, and
- allocating resources (such as materials), costs and people against tasks.

In addition to those issues, a realistic forecast of fee income must be maintained to provide information for managing the practice's existing and expected work-load so that action to recruit (or otherwise) design or other staff can be taken as necessary.

It is also necessary to investigate the causes of job overruns. The fee quotation or time estimate may have been unrealistic, or the balance of staff assigned to the project may have been inappropriate or their performance inadequate. It may be that work additional to the original commission has 'crept' in. Whatever the reason, the lessons must be learned.

TABLE A.1: *Commercial time and cost management systems for architects*

ArchiOffice	Orange Loft LLC (Chicago US) www.archioffice.com
framework2009	Software (Europe) Ltd 01522 881 300 www.framework-software.com
Paprika	01732 811 600 www.paprika-software.com

Appendix B
In-house project management

Work stage planning

The cycle of work within a work stage, which has the objective of launching the next stage, is:

- stating the objective and assimilation of relevant facts
- assessment and provision of resources required
- planning the work and setting timetables
- carrying out work
- making proposals and reporting progress, and
- making decisions; setting objectives for the next stage.

Project programmes

At commencement, prepare a project programme to show the period for each work stage and any critical dates. At the end of each work stage review the programme to co-ordinate the consequences of change or delay, the timing of activities during the next stage and the information required, including any outstanding work.

Progress and work stage reports

At the end of each stage, prepare a report setting out the proposals, current cost estimate and actual or potential changes to the level of detail appropriate to that work stage and seeking approval to commence the next work stage.

Maintaining control

Efficiency and cost-effectiveness can be improved if:

- a plan of work is established at the beginning and used to regulate and co-ordinate activities in conjunction with the project procedures
- client and designers agree to freeze the brief at the end of Work Stage D and the design (or content of the employer's requirements) at the end of Work Stage E
- if all concerned take the required actions at the correct times.

It cannot be over-emphasised that the greater the number of unplanned departures from information previously issued to others for action, the greater the risk of loss of control and abortive work.

Handover

A successful project will include plans for the client to take over the project, which should be as detailed as other strategies in the procurement process. Occupation can be stressful – nothing is the same or in the same place as it used to be. This problem can be minimised if the architect provides a structured transfer of information over the first few months – 'initial occupation' services at Work Stage L2. The beneficial impact on the occupation/settling-in process will be immediately apparent.

Apart from any other issues in the context of fees alone, if the post-handover process is not properly planned and managed, the architect may incur unrecoverable costs.

Appendix C
Managing time and cost

The crucial management tool in job costing is the time sheet. Principals and all staff – professional, technical and administrative – should be required to complete time sheets. It is never easy to persuade staff of the need to complete time sheets, which is often seen as a tiresome chore imposed on busy people who consider they are already doing their best. Staff are more likely to comply if care is taken to explain why time sheets are needed – particularly if it is pointed out that they are a mechanism to provide valuable information about the underlying costs of providing a professional service, which can be used to improve efficiency and profitability, all of which will bring benefits for the staff themselves.

"Time spent on a job can be measured, but arithmetic says nothing about how effectively that time has been spent"

Calculating the cost of time

To establish the cost of employment of the fee-earning personnel, including principals, professionals and technologists in the office, data can be collected from a number of different sources:

- from weekly time sheets (see Figure C.1)
- the number of project-specific, fee-earning hours expressed as a percentage of total available hours (see Figure C.3)
- from practice financial records. The cost of employing each professional will include salary, bonus, employer's National Insurance contributions, benefits (car, pension, private health, training, etc.), and indirect costs such as salaries

of administrative staff, professional indemnity and other insurances and all other costs of running the business that are not specifically project-related, together with costs such as accommodation, utilities, consumables, travel, fees and charges. The indirect costs are usually, but not always, shared evenly between all personnel (see column 3 of Figure C.4)

- the weighted or real cost of each fee-earning hour, plus an appropriate margin (see column 7 of Figure C.4).

This data can also be used as part of the practice's annual business plan review. Nevertheless, it is important to remember that time spent on a job can be measured, but arithmetic says nothing about how effectively that time has been spent.

The simple system described below has been developed from ideas in *The Handbook* and demonstrates the principles and necessary outputs for a time and cost elements analysis of the practice's management processes.

The components of this system are the time sheets (Figure C.1), their analysis (Figure C.3) and the calculations of the cost of fee-earning hours (Figure C.4).

Name Phil Webb		Date	14 05 XX	Week 7		IVOR B'ARCH Architects Time sheet		
Job no.	Work Stage	Monday	Tuesday	Wednesday	Thursday	Friday	Total	Overtime
4/192	EF	7.5	7.5	4.5	3	3	25.5	
4/150	K	0	0	0	4.5	0	4.5	
4/150	AS/VO23	0	0	0	0	2.5	2.5	
		0	0	0	0	0	0	
		0	0	0	0	0	0	
	Marketing	0	0	0	0	0	0	
	Administration	0	0	0	0	1	1	
	CPD	0	0	4	0	0	4	
Leave incl. sick leave		0	0	0	0	0	0	
	Totals	7.5	7.5	8.5	7.5	6.5	**37.5**	

Notes *Working day – 7.5 hours   Minimum time unit – 15 minutes = 0.25*
Overtime work and overtime rates must be agreed beforehand.
*If providing an **additional service** under 'Work Stage' enter 'AS' followed by identification reference for the work. Phrases such as 'altering drawings' or 'drawing work' or 'attending meetings' may prove woefully inadequate in a formal dispute tribunal.*

FIGURE C.1: *Example time sheet*

Hours per year			
	52 weeks × 5 working days × 7.5 hours/day		1,950
less	Public holidays	8 × 7.5	60	
	Paid holiday	20 × 7.5	150	
	Sick leave (say)		40	250
	Total available hours			**1,700**
		Total per month (say)		140

FIGURE C.2: *Available hours*

Time sheet data (and the cost of a fee-earning hour) might be analysed twice a year and/or when the number of professionals and technologists changes. In the absence of sufficient historical data, or for simplicity, it may be necessary to complete the analysis of time sheets on a 'best guess' basis and the relevant numbers entered into Figure C.4. The numbers in Figures C.3 and C.4 were completed on this basis, and it was assumed that each person works about 1,700 hours a year or 140 hours per month (see Figure C.4).

It is interesting to note that the Association of Consulting Engineers suggests that the number of effective (fee-earning) hours might be deemed to be 1,600 hours without further deductions (October 2003).

In the larger practice it may be simpler and more realistic to regard the full cost of the principals' time as a practice overhead if most is spent on management and marketing. Nevertheless, principals should always fill in time sheets; it will be a bonus if they also earn fees.

20XX	Projects		Marketing		Administration		CPD		
Name	Hours	%	Hours	%	Hours	%	Hours	%	
I. B'Arch	90		20		27		3		140 hours
		64		14		19		2	100%
C. Wren	110		5		21		4		140 hours
		79		3		15		3	100%
I. Jones	125		0		11		4		140 hours
		89		0		8		3	100%
P. Webb	125		0		11		4		140 hours
		89		0		8		3	100%

FIGURE C.3: *Analysis of time sheet data to show usage by staff/grade*

	1	2	3	4	5	6	7	8
Year	Basic salary	Direct employment costs	Indirect costs	Total cost p.a.	Fee-earning % of time	Fee-earning hours p.a.	Cost per fee-earning hour	Add 20% margin
20XX	£	£	£	£	%	Hours	£	£
I. B'Arch[a]	35,000	10,000	30,000	75,000	64	1,088	69	83
C. Wren	35,000	8,000	30,000	73,000	79	1,343	54	65
I. Jones	28,000	5,000	30,000	63,000	89	1,513	42	50
P. Webb	24,000	4,000	30,000	58,000	89	1,513	38	46

Column 4 is the sum of columns 1, 2 and 3
Column 5 is derived from Figure C.3
Column 6 is the column 5 percentage of 1,700 hours
Column 7 is column 4 divided by column 6
Column 8 adds 20 per cent margin to column 7
[a] Always agree a notional basic salary for each principal for application as necessary when calculating a fee offer.

FIGURE C.4: *Calculating the cost of a fee-earning hour*

Solo practitioners

A solo practitioner, i.e. with no employees, working from a home-office will approach this exercise from a different perspective, but the process will be the same. The basic information necessary to calculate the direct and indirect costs will be identified in book-keeping records or annual accounts, such as those required for income tax purposes. The first matter to be decided is a realistic target for the annual return (which, of course, would include the profit element but exclude reimbursable expenses).

For instance, if the desired return is £40,000 per year before income tax and National Insurance with overheads of, say, £20,000, then:

1   working a 35-hour week of which, say, five hours are non-fee-earning would require an average rate of about *£42* per hour,

2   if working hours are increased by working nine-hour days, making no allowance for illness and taking 15 days' holiday, the average rate would drop to about *£30* per fee-earning hour, or

Fee-earning potential 20XX	1,088	£83	£90,000	*col. 6 × col. 8*
	1,343	£65	£87,600	*do*
	1,513	£50	£75,600	*do*
	1,513	£46	£69,600	*do*
			£322,800	
Assessment of fee income [a]		90%		£290,520
Salary costs excluding principal		*col. 1*	£87,000	
Other costs		*col. 2*	£27,000	
		col. 3	£120,000	£234,000
Profit including principal's 'salary'				**£56,520**

[a] Fee income should be assessed on the basis of market conditions and expressed as a percentage of the maximum potential income. In this example, 90 per cent is the equivalent of:

- assuming difficulty in obtaining sufficient commissions, or
- cutting the profit margin from (wished for) 20 per cent to 10 per cent, or
- providing a buffer for poor financial returns – job overruns, client dissatisfaction or similar situations, or
- any of the above in combination.

Alternatively, the 10 per cent could be a potential fund to provide bonus payments for good performance and for special marketing efforts to close the perceived gap in potential.

FIGURE C.5: *Business planning using Figure C.4 data*

3   if another occupation, such as teaching part-time (or sailing), would restrict the available time to 1,000 fee-earning hours, i.e. excluding time for book-keeping, invoicing, etc., the rate would have to be:
- *£60*, although this might be unsustainable; but
- reducing the rate to *£30* per hour and overheads to £10,000, would give an annual return of about £20,000 before tax and National Insurance.

In the worked example (Appendix D, Figure D.3, page 109) the total number of hours for Stages C to L (for the principal and employees) is 212 and the fee amounts to 12 per cent of the cost of construction. Assuming the same number of hours by the solo practitioner and applying the rates above for an annual return of £40,000, the equivalent fee would be:

- @ £42 = £8,904 or *9%* + about *four* other projects of a similar size to achieve the target return
- @ £30 = £6,360 or *7%* + *five* or *six* other projects
- @ £60 = £12,720 or *13%* + *two* or *three* other projects
- @ £30 = £6,360 or *7%* + *three* or *four* other projects (for annual return of £20,000).

Appendix D
Calculating the resources

The resources required are time, appropriate professionals and technologists, managerial and administrative back-up, accommodation, equipment and money.

This section seeks to demonstrate the principles for estimating the professional and technical staff time required to complete a commission, calculating the cost of those resources and their relation to the proposed fee.

The planning tool

The methodology proposed, developed from an idea by Michael Brown RIBA, uses a planning tool in three parts – the resource calculation sheets, the fee proposal and the resource cost plan with fee comparison.

The demonstration model is a relatively simple spreadsheet in Microsoft Excel comprising:

- protected cells, shaded grey, containing formulae which automatically display totals or other results and transfer them to the resource cost plan for comparison with the fee proposal
- unprotected cells into which the user enters the activities and other project data, e.g. hours for each activity, hourly rates or provision for expenses.

The spreadsheet can be kept as the master file and copies made as required.

For the demonstration, the services outlined in the RIBA Conditions of Appointment for a Domestic Project and the schedule Services for a Small Project are used as a basis for the example in Figure D.1 sheets 1–3 for reasons of simplicity. However, the principles apply equally to projects of all sizes using RIBA Agreements or any other agreement with the client.

Resource calculation sheets

Figure D.1 provides for systematic assessment and measurement of the work content, based on the staged provision of information, drawings, schedules and specifications, and/or the estimated number of hours required.

The estimated number of drawings required is entered in the relevant column and an appropriate number of hours allocated by staff grade. In Figure D.1 sheet 3 this column is for recording the anticipated number of hours required for each month of the construction phase; the entry under the staff category is a multiple of the monthly requirement and the number of months.

In addition to the time allowed for preparing drawings and related information, time must also be allowed for their development or revision. Preliminary schedules of drawings can be prepared, perhaps structured along the lines suggested in *CPI Co-ordinated Project Information* (Building Project Information Committee, 2003).

At least one practice has calculated from historical data the cost of preparing each size of drawing, including an allowance for development and revision. This is used in conjunction with the preliminary schedules and the average hourly cost of the office to provide a rough check on the number of hours required.

If work stage related data is available from practice records, it is not necessary to complete all lines. Instead, for each work stage enter the estimated number of hours required in a single line.

Resource cost plan

When the data on hourly costs excluding profit is entered into Figure D.2, the net cost of providing the services/resources is calculated and displayed automatically.

Fee calculation

For each work stage the estimated duration of the stage, the estimated cost of construction and the basic fee, expressed as the percentage payable on completion of the stage, are entered by the user into Figure D.3, together with a notional hourly rate including profit in the 'other fees' section and the notional percentage to create a budget for expenses. The results of these entries will be automatically displayed. At this stage the decision about the percentage for the fee is made empirically.

The consequences are shown concurrently with the resource costs and the proposed fee in Figure D.4. If the comparison of costs with the basic fee shows an unsustainable imbalance, the proposed fee or the entries in the unprotected cells can be adjusted and the new results reviewed. If this exercise still shows that the risks to the practice are unacceptable then the invitation to submit a fee must reluctantly be declined.

Time-based basic fee

If the whole fee is time based, the budget for each stage will be the same as the costs shown in Figure D.3, to which must be added the profit element. Figures D.2 and D.4 are not relevant in this case.

Other services

If an 'other service' is to be provided, i.e. not included in the basic fee, a brief description and an estimate of the number of hours required is entered in the time charges column in Figure D.1. These services will normally be subject to additional time charges. The number of hours is totalled and transferred to the resource cost plan, Figure D.2. If an additional service is to be included in the basic fee, the time is entered in the ordinary way.

Expenses

In the resource cost plan, any special expenses (for example, the fee of a structural engineer) are entered, together with a notional percentage of the fee for project-related expenses. This percentage is used whether or not expenses are to be recharged. Travel time should be included in the resource calculation sheets for visits away from the architect's office.

Monitoring resource costs

Figure D.5 demonstrates how performance costs can be compared with the current fee and how they relate to the original plan (Figure D.2). In the example it has been assumed that hourly costs have been increased and that the estimated cost of the project was reduced.

Using the schedules in communications with the client

In Section 5 it was noted that *'the information about the fee itself is most easily conveyed using a fee management schedule'* and that *'for smaller projects it may be feasible to describe the offer within the text of a letter.'*

A fee management schedule (Figure D.6) can be created using the data displayed in Figure D.3. This schedule can be used throughout the project to track changes in fee outcomes for the architect's (and client's) information.

In any negotiations to reduce the fee, the resource calculation sheets (Figure D.1) can be used to demonstrate what is offered and what could be left out.

In many cases the offer can be made using a fee schedule (Figure D.7), or in words in a letter (Figure D.8).

Figure D.7 is an electronically customised and completed document based on the RIBA's on-line Schedule of Fees and Expenses.

PLAN OF WORK DOMESTIC PROJECT Job No.: 09/016 Prepared: 00 12 XX	Time charges	Number of drawings	Principal	I. Jones	C. Wren	P. Webb	Hours in Basic Fee
Before construction							
Initial meeting with client	0		3	0	0	0	3
Fee letter (feasibility)	0		1	0	0	0	1
Preparation							
Visit the property and carry out initial appraisal	3	0	0	0	0	0	0
Assist the client to prepare the client's requirements	3	0	0	0	0	0	0
Identify alternative solutions for the project	15	2	0	0	0	0	0
Client meeting re. feasibility studies, time and cost	4	0	0	0	0	0	0
Calculate resources and fee proposal	0	0	4	0	0	0	4
Explain terms of appointment and fee proposal	0	0	0	0	0	0	0
Advise on need for consultants or specialists	1	0	0	0	0	0	0
Minutes of meeting	1	0	0	0	0	0	0
Total Appraisal and briefing	27		8	0	0	0	8
Design							
Letter of Appointment with RIBA Conditions	0	0	2	0	0	0	2
Photographic/measured surveys	14	0	0	0	0	0	0
Arrange soil investigation and report	n/a	0	0	0	0	0	0
Analyse brief. Prepare outline proposals	0	2	2	0	7	2	11
Consultations with planners, consultants, etc.	0	0	0	0	4	0	4
Client meeting re. preliminary design, time and cost	0	0	3	0	0	0	3
Minutes of meeting	0	0	1	0	0	0	1
Develop the final design	0	2	2	0	7	7	16
Prepare approximate estimate of cost	0	QS	0	0	0	0	0
Meeting to agree final design proposals, time and cost	0	0	3	0	0	0	3
Meeting to agree landlord/neighbour negotiations	0	0	1	0	0	0	1
Minutes of meeting	0	0	1	0	0	0	1
Prepare and submit planning application	0	1	0	0	3	2	5
Further survey	0		0	0	0	0	0
Set up consultant appointments	2		0	0	0	0	0
Prepare interior design scheme including furniture	24		0	0	0	0	0
Visits to showrooms and other projects with client	20		0	0	0	0	0
Total Design proposals	60		15	0	21	11	47

Include travelling time where appropriate

FIGURE D.1: *Resource calculation sheet 1*

PLAN OF WORK DOMESTIC PROJECT Job No.: 09/016 Prepared: 00 12 XX	Time charges	Number of drawings	Principal	I. Jones	C. Wren	P. Webb	Hours in Basic Fee
Exceptional negotiations with planners	0						
Negotiations with landlord, neighbours, etc.	0						
Adjustment of design if required	0						
Re-submit for approval if required	0						
Construction information							
Prepare/agree schedules of finishes, etc.	0	4	3	0	0	7	10
Prepare location, assembly & component drwgs	0	6	1	0	14	7	22
Prepare location drawings showing services	0	1	0	0	0	7	7
Prepare schedules of joinery, ironmongery, etc.	0	0	0	0	0	7	7
Integrate design information by others	0	0	0	0	0	0	0
Make calculations required under Bldg Regs	0	0	0	0	4	3	7
Prepare/make submission for Bldg Regs	0	0	0	0	2	2	4
Prepare Specification/Schedule of Works	0	0	1	0	0	14	15
Total Construction information	0		5	0	20	47	72
CONSTRUCTION STAGES							
Tender action							
Advise on building contract and responsibilities arising	0	0	2	0	0	0	2
Advise client to arrange insurance for alterations, etc.	0	0	1	0	0	0	1
Advise on invitation of tenders and tenderers	0	0	2	0	0	0	2
Prepare and issue tender documents	0	0	0	0	2	2	4
Arrange access for tenderers	0	0	0	0	0	0	0
Receive tenders, appraise and report to client	0	0	2	0	0	0	2
Amend construction information if tender sum adjusted	0						
Total Tender action	0		7	0	2	2	11

The notional project, on which the worked example is based, is for work to the client's home. In consequence, the client is exempt from the CDM Regulations (and certain other legislation) and no provision for co-ordinating the work of other consultants is required.

The client is seeking an extension and alterations to a high standard but is not clear about the available options and asked the architect, prior to entering the formal agreement, to prepare feasibility studies and develop the brief (Work Stage AB) on the basis of time charges.

FIGURE D.1: *Resource calculation sheet 2*

PLAN OF WORK DOMESTIC PROJECT Job No.: 09/016 Prepared: 00 12 XX	Time charges	Hours per month	Principal	I. Jones	C. Wren	P. Webb	Hours in Basic Fee
Construction work	Duration	4					
Advise client on appointment of a builder	0		3	0	0	0	3
Prepare contract documents & arrange signing	0		1	0	2	0	3
Issue information required for construction	0		0	0	0	2	2
Administer the terms of the building contract	0	Included below	0	0	0	0	0
Issue further information and instructions	0	2	1	0	4	3	8
Site visits at agreed intervals	0	4	0	0	12	4	16
Minutes of meetings	0	1	0	0	2	2	4
Value work carried out	0	QS	0	0	0	0	0
Issue interim certificates	0	1	2	0	2	0	4
Issue monthly report to client	0	1	0	0	4	0	4
Arrange commissioning of services installations	0		0	0	0	2	2
Inspect works at completion	0		3	0	0	4	7
Check that all snagging defects remedied	0		0	0	0	3	3
Provide or obtain record drawings	0		0	0	0	2	2
Agree defects reporting procedure	0		1	0	0	0	1
Issue completion certificate & interim valuation	0		2	0	0	0	2
Prepare and issue information for client variations	20						
Total Construction	20		13	0	26	22	61
After handover							
Advise on necessary action for defects			0	0	2	2	4
Draft final account/agree with contractor		QS	0	0	0	0	0
Pre-final inspection of Works			0	0	0	3	3
Agree programme for remedial works			0	0	1	0	1
Final inspection. Issue certificate of m.g. defects			1	0	2	0	3
(Receive final account and) issue Final Certificate			2	0	0	0	2
Advise on matters outside the architect's control	0						
Total After completion	0		3	0	5	5	13
Advise client that architect's services are complete							
Total hours all stages excluding additional services			51	0	74	87	212

FIGURE D.1: *Resource calculation sheet 3*

RESOURCE COST DOMESTIC PROJECT Prepared: 00 12 XX		Job No.: 09/016		Principal	I. Jones	C. Wren	P. Webb	
Work Stages			£/hour*	£69	£54	£42	£38	
AB	*Preparation*		Hours	8	0	0	0	
£/hr = cost excluding profit			Cost	£552	£0	£0	£0	£552
CD	*Design*		Hours	15	0	21	11	
			Cost	£1,035	£0	£882	£418	£2,335
EF	*Construction info.*		Hours	5	0	20	47	
			Cost	£345	£0	£840	£1,786	£2,971
GH	*Tender action*		Hours	7	0	2	2	
			Cost	£483	£0	£84	£76	£643
JK	*Construction*		Hours	13	0	26	22	
			Cost	£897	£0	£1,092	£836	£2,825
L	*After handover*		Hours	3	0	5	5	
			Cost	£207	£0	£210	£190	£607
Other Fees								£9,933
Provisional allocation			Hours	30	0	41	30	
			Cost	£2,070	£0	£1,722	£1,140	£4,932
		Total staff costs						£14,865

Expenses

Special expenses:	*Structural Engineer*	£250
	(QS by Client)	£0
		£0
Expenses as % of staff costs	5%	£743
Total expenses		£993

Gross cost	**£15,858**

Estimated total fee from fee proposal	£20,092

Variation	**£4,234**

FIGURE D.2: *Resource cost plan*

	Duration months	Basic Fee option[a]	Basic Fee[b]	Construction cost: £k	Estimated total fee: £	Estimated resource cost
FEE CALCULATION **DOMESTIC PROJECT** Job No.: 09/016 **Prepared: 00 12 XX**						
Basic Fees						
AB *Preparation*	2	T	0%	100	0	£552
CD *Design*	2	CLS	3.5%	100	3,500	£2,335
EF *Construction info.*	2	CLS	3.5%	100	3,500	£2,971
GH *Tender action*	1	CLS	0.5%	100	500	£643
JK *Construction*	4	CLS	4%	100	4,000	£2,825
L *After handover*	6	CLS	0.5%	100	500	£607
Alternative All stages	0	0%	0		0	
Total work stage fees		12%			£12,000	£9,933

Other Fees: @   £65   notional rate/hour[c]

Preparation		27	£1,755			
Design		60	£3,900			
Construction info.		0	£0			
Tender action		0	£0			
Construction		20	£1,300			
After handover		0	£0			
Provisional budget for additional services		107			£6,955	£4,932
			Sub-total		£18,955	

Expenses, etc.   Budget[d]   6%   £1,137

[a] Basic Fee percentage [%]   Fixed lump sum [FLS]
    Calculated lump sum [CLS] or Time [T]
[b] Basic Fee expressed as % of construction cost
[c] Notional hourly rate including profit
[d] As % of fee. Enter 0 if expenses are not charged

Estimated total fee	£20,092	£15,858
VAT @ 17.5%	£3,516	
	£23,608	

FIGURE D.3: *Fee calculation*

RESOURCE COST AND FEES COMPARED	JOB No.: 09/016					
Prepared: 00 12 XX	**Stages**	**Cost**	%[a]	**Fee**	%[a]	
	Preparation	£552	0.6	£0	0.0	
	Design	£2,335	2.3	£3,500	3.5	
	Construction info.	£2,971	3.0	£3,500	3.5	
	Tender action	£643	0.6	£500	0.5	
	Construction	£2,825	2.8	£4,000	4.0	
	After handover	£607	0.6	£500	0.5	
	Totals of work stages	£9,933	9.9	£12,000	12.0	
Variation excluding Other Fees and expenses		£1,600	17	(profit on Basic Fee)		

[a] % of construction cost

FIGURE D.4: *Resource costs and fee proposal compared*

RESOURCE MONITOR DOMESTIC PROJECT Job No.: 09/016 Prepared: 00 12 XX			*Principal*	*I. Jones*	*C. Wren*	*P. Webb*	Current cost	Current fee incl. profit	Variation fee − cost	Initial cost plan
AB	Preparation	Rate	£69	£54	£42	£38				
		Hours	6	0	0	0	£414	£0	−£414	£552
		AS[a]	8	0	0	0	£552	£662	£110	£1,755
CD	Design	Rate	£69	£54	£42	£38				
		Hours	10	10	20	0	£2,070	£3,500	£1,430	£2,335
		AS	22	7	14	0	£2,484	£3,523	£1,039	£3,900
JK	Construction	Rate	**£69**	**£60**	**£45**	**£40**				
	information	Hours	6	0	25	40	£3,139	£3,500	£361	£2,971
		AS	0	0	5	0	£225	£270	£45	£0
GH	Tender action	Rate	£0	£0	£0	£0				
		Hours	0	0	0	0	£0	£0	£0	£643
		AS	0	0	0	0	£0	£0	£0	£0
JK	Construction	Rate	£0	£0	£0	£0				
		Hours	0	0	0	0	£0	£0	£0	£2,825
		AS	0	0	0	0	£0	£0	£0	£1,300
L	After handover	Rate	£0	£0	£0	£0				
		Hours	0	0	0	0	£0	£0	£0	£607
		AS	0	0	0	0	£0	£0	£0	£0
							£5,623	£11,455	£2,571	£16,888

[a] Additional services
Time sheet data is entered in this work sheet on completion of each work stage.
Rates are entered each time to cover increases.
Current fees from schedule [see fee accounts].

FIGURE D.5: *Resource monitor*

Basic Fees	Basic Fee option[a]	Fee basis	Works cost: £k	Estimated total fee: £	Duration months	Account basis
IVOR B'ARCH Architects LLP						RIBA Chartered Practice
Project: *Alterations at 16 Private Crescent*						
Job no. *09/016*						
Fee management plan						
Issue 2			Date *15 06 XX*			
Before construction stages						
AB Preparation	T	n/a	0	0	2	See Other Fees
CD Design	CLS	3.5%	100	3,500	2	Billed monthly
EF Construction info.	CLS	4%	100	3,500	2	Billed monthly
Construction stages						
GH Tender action	CLS	0.5%	100	500	1	Billed monthly
JK Construction	CLS	4%	100	4,000	4	Billed monthly
L After handover	CLS	0.5%	100	500	6	Billed monthly
Total Basic Fee		12.0%		£12,000	17	(11 months + 6)

Other Fees as fee proposal	Hours	£ – notional rate		
Preparation	27	65	1,755	Billed as earned
Additional services as required	80	65	5,200	Billed as earned
	0	0	0	
Other Fee budget			£6,955	
Total fees			£18,955	

Expenses budget	@	6%	of fees	£1,137
				£20,092
VAT	@	17.5%		£3,516
				£23,608
			say	**£24,000**

This plan is for budgetary purposes only. Actual fees and expenses will reflect the services performed in accordance with the Agreement.

[a] Basic Fee options:
Percentage [%], fixed lump sum [FLS], calculated lump sums [CLS], time [T]

FIGURE D.6: *A fee management schedule*

RIBA Schedule of Fees and Expenses

Basic Fee

As Designer

Clause	Stage		Fee	
5.6	A	Appraisal	Time	] budget £10,000
5.6	B	Design brief	Time	]
5.5.3	C	Concept	1.2%*	
5.5.3	D	Design development	1.2%*	
5.5.3	E	Technical design	0.9%*	
5.5.3	F	Production information	1.2%*	
5.5.3	G	Tender documentation	0.12%*	
5.5.3	H	Tender action	0.06%*	
5.5.3	J	Mobilisation	Time	
5.6	K	Construction to completion	Time	
5.6	L1	Post practical completion	Time	
5.5.1	L2	Assist building users	£2,500 (C. Wren × 35 hours max)	

* As Lead Consultant, Lead Designer and Contract Administrator relevant stage fee increased by 10% (percentage fees only)

Other Fees

Other fees are fees for any 'Other Services' not included in the Basic Fee and if applicable any licence fee

Clause	Ref. no.		Fee	
5.6	3a–c	Design brief	Time	Budget £5,000
5.6	7	Negotiations statutory approvals	Time over 5 hours	
5.5.1	9	Accessibility audit	£3,000	

	Person/grade	Rate	Person/grade	Rate
Time charges	I. B'Arch	£100/hour	I. Jones	£50/hour
	C. Wren	£78/hour	P. Webb	£46/hour

FIGURE D.7: *Example of a RIBA schedule completed electronically*

Expenses and disbursements

The specified expenses listed below are charged
in addition to the fees at net cost plus a handling charge of   8   %

Specified expenses

Black and white paper copies of drawings and documents

Electronic copies in 'read only' format

Travel, hotel expenses and subsistence payments

Other expenses and disbursements made on
behalf of the Client[a] will be charged at net cost   3   %
plus

Where applicable, travel is charged at   40p   per mile

Rates for black and white paper copies

	A4	A3	A2	A1	AO
Printing	15p	30p	£1.40	£2.40	£3.40
Plotting	£4.00	£6.00	£10.00	£15.00	£30.00

Payment

VAT Registration number of the payee is: 987 6543-21

Instalments of fees to be calculated and paid on the basis of the estimate of the
percentage of completion of the Services or stages or additional services or such
other method specified below:

Y   by monthly instalments

*The (estimated) Basic Fee for Stages C and D and for E–H will be calculated and divided into
instalments equal to their planned duration in months plus 1 and recalculated at the end of
each stage.*

[a] Such as payments to the local authority for planning submissions or Building Regulations approval.

FIGURE D.7: *Example of a RIBA schedule completed electronically (continued)*

Our fees for the services in the schedule will be:

- for the design stage: [__ % of the building cost] [a lump sum of £ __]
- for the construction information stage: [__ % of the building cost] [a lump sum of £ __]
- for the construction stages: [time charges] [__ % of the building cost, which includes for [*number of*] visits to the site in connection with our duties during construction]

The latter includes for [*number of*] visits to the site in connection with our duties during construction.

Services identified by 'T' in the schedule and any extra services will be charged at £ __ per hour where performed by a partner and at £ __ where performed by other staff. For such services we will obtain your consent before providing more than __ hours in the 'before construction' stages and __ hours in the construction stages.

Before implementing any changes to the services or design we will agree with you any consequential change to our fee.

[Our fee includes our expenses.] [In addition to the fee the following expenses will be charged [at net cost] [plus a handling charge of __ %] [by the addition of __ % to the total fee]

[list expenses]

Any disbursements made on your behalf, such as payments to the local authority for planning submissions or Building Regulations approval will be charged at net cost [plus a handling charge of __ %]

[We are registered for VAT, which is chargeable on all fees and expenses.] [VAT is not chargeable on our accounts as we are not registered, but if during the course of this appointment it is necessary to register for VAT this will change.]

FIGURE D.8: *Specimen fee offer described in words*

Appendix E
Fee accounts and VAT

The simple format of accounts and VAT invoices shown in Figures E.1 to E.5 are intended only to demonstrate the principles. Commercial software packages are available for invoicing, some of which include links to records of project resource usage – time and cost.

> *See also:*
> *Appendix A,*
> *Figure A.1,*
> *page 91*

The fee account

The first important principle is to submit accounts promptly and regularly. Accounts for unexpected large sums may cause embarrassment to the client and consequent delay, if not worse, in payment.

"Submit accounts promptly and regularly"

The next issue is to ensure that invoices are compatible with and issued in accordance with the client's procedures. Owen Luder has provided helpful advice on this subject, reproduced in *Making payment easy* on page 119.

The information which is necessary to obtain a payment from the client and for the VAT requirements of client and/or architect comprises:

- the fees and expenses due at the date of application, less any previous payments, and
- any VAT due on the balance, plus
- any disbursements made on behalf of the client, and
- the total amount payable excluding tax, and
- the total amount of tax chargeable.

Figures E.2 to E.5 demonstrate a simple spreadsheet system for fees accounts, and back-up calculations, perhaps using data automatically transferred from the time and resource systems.

Figure E.2 establishes the base data for all fee calculations. In the example, the basic fee uses the calculated lump sum option and the works cost has been reduced for Work Stage EF following a more accurate estimate at the end of the previous stage (see Figure E.3). Further amendments can be made to the following stages as the cost is refined.

This document, excluding the cash-flow calculations, might be used to support the fee offer in the initial discussions with the client.

Once the project is underway, the cumulative schedule of fee and expenses (Figure E.2) can be used to demonstrate progress and the basis of the current fee account (Figure E.3). In the example, a transcription error occurred and, to correct the situation, a credit/debit note is used (Figure E.5).

Whether the client is sent copies of the supporting schedules is a matter of judgement. That may not be appropriate for a domestic project as used here for demonstration purposes, but a reactive methodology is still necessary to demonstrate the true current financial status in the context of the future commitments of the project.

If the supporting schedules are sent to the client, they will not form part of the VAT invoice, but it will be a 'related document' and a copy should be attached to the copy of the VAT invoice for future reference.

Making payment easy

from *Keeping Out of Trouble* by Owen Luder (page 29)

Establish at the earliest possible stage your client's system for paying accounts. Organise the timing of your fee applications to match your client's accounts department's procedures for paying bills. If they pay on the first day of the month and you send your account in on the second, you will not get paid that month!

Establish if they have a BACS system for making payments, and if so make sure they have your correct bank account details and inform them if these change for any reason. However, you may not notice when you have not been paid – you do not have the prompt of paying a cheque into your bank. Do check that the BACS payments are being made on time, and that when paid they are recorded on the fee file.

With private clients, in particular, establish how they are funding the project and your fees. If they are raising a mortgage, establish with them in advance estimated amounts and timing of interim fee payments so that they can budget accordingly. A significant part of your fees will be due before building starts and they may overlook this.

Have a system to ensure you submit your accounts the moment they are due. If you have not sent an account to your client you cannot get paid!

Find out who will be responsible for approving your accounts and passing them for payment. This is the person you need to know well enough to make direct contact with when there are any problems or delays with fee payments.

You must also have a system for chasing unpaid accounts the moment they are overdue. It is good tactics for the initial payment chaser to be someone other than you. Keep it impersonal until the situation gets so difficult that you need to become involved.

Get your fee accounts out on time and in tune with your client's payments system, and have a system for chasing them if they are not paid on time.

1 July 20X2

Dear Mr and Mrs Homeowner

Alterations to 16 Private Crescent

We enclose our application for payment of fee account number <u>5</u> in the sum of £3,330.92 together with a copy of:

- the updated fee management plan;
- the cumulative schedule of fees earned;
- the cumulative schedule of expenses;
- the cumulative schedule of disbursements.

as appropriate

You will note that our fees have been adjusted to reflect <u>reduction in the estimated cost of construction to</u> £98,400 reported to you on 10 June.

Please note that payment is due within 14 days of the application date shown on the account. The account is not a tax invoice. A VAT invoice will be issued on receipt of payment.

~~May we respectfully draw your attention to the statement of account, which shows that £_____ is outstanding. You will be aware that Clause 5.13 in our agreement provides for interest on late payments.~~ [*For use with discretion*]

Yours faithfully

Ivor B'Arch

for and on behalf of Ivor B'Arch Architects LLP

FIGURE E.1: *Model letter to client with fee account*

IVOR B'ARCH Architects LLP

RIBA ⬦
Chartered Practice

Project: *Alterations at 16 Private Crescent*

Job no.   *09/016*

Fee management plan

Issue   **2**   Date   *15 06 X2*

Basic Fees		Basic Fee option[a]	Fee basis	Works cost: £k	Estimated total fee: £	Duration: months	Account basis
Before construction stages							
AB	*Preparation*	T	*n/a*	*0.0*	0	2	*See Other Fees*
CD	*Design*	CLS	*3.5%*	*100*	*3,500*	2	*Billed monthly*
EF	*Construction info.*	CLS	*3.5%*	*94.8*	*3,318*	2	*Billed monthly*
Construction stages					*Transcription error*		
GH	*Tender action*	CLS	*0.5%*	*94.8*	*474*	1	*Billed monthly*
JK	*Construction*	CLS	*4.0%*	*94.8*	*3,792*	4	*Billed monthly*
L	*After handover*	CLS	*0.5%*	*94.8*	*474*	6	*Billed monthly*

Total Basic Fee			12%		£11,558	17	(11 months + 6)

Other Fees as fee proposal	Hours	£ – notional rate		
Preparation	27	65.00	1,755	*Billed as earned*
Additional services as required	80	65.00	5,200	*Billed as earned*
	0	0.00	0	

	Other Fee budget	£6,955
	Total fees	£18,513

Expenses budget	@	6%	of fees	£1,111
				£19,624
VAT	@	17.5%		£3,434
				£23,058
			say	**£23,000**

> This plan is for budgetary purposes only. Actual fees and expenses will reflect the services performed in accordance with the Agreement.

[a] Basic Fee options:
Percentage [%], fixed lump sum [FLS], calculated lump sums [CLS], time [T]

FIGURE E.2: *Fee management plan*
Note   The fee management plan should be reviewed at the end of each work stage or every five to six months.

	Stage	Duration:	Basic Fee	Other Fee	Expenses		VAT 17.5%	Totals	Payment
Cash flow					Provisional plan dependent on progress				
Issue *2*	Date	*15 06 X2*			Payments to be made before end of following month				
20XX		months	£	£	£	£	£	£	due
Jan.			0	0	0	0	0	**0**	
Feb.	*AB*	2	*T*	705	42	747	131	**878**	Mar.
Mar.	*AB*		*T*	662	40	702	123	**825**	Apr.
Apr.	*CD*	2	*1,750*	0	105	1,855	325	**2,180**	May
May	*CD*		*1,750*	3,523	316	5,589	978	**6,568**	Jun.
Jun.	*EF*	2	*1,659*	270	116	2,045	359	**2,404**	Jul.
Jul.	*EF*		*1,659*	0	100	1,759	308	**2,066**	Aug.
Aug.	*GH*	1	*474*	0	28	502	88	**590**	Sept.
Sept.	*JK*	4	*948*	1,000	117	2,065	361	**2,426**	Oct.
Oct.	*JK*		*948*	1,200	129	2,277	398	**2,675**	Nov.
Nov.	*JK*		*948*	0	57	1,005	176	**1,181**	Dec.
Dec.	*JK*		*948*	0	57	1,005	176	**1,181**	Jan.
20X2									
Jan.			0	0	0	0	0	**0**	Feb.
Feb.			0	0	0	0	0	**0**	Mar.
Mar.	*L*	3	*237*	0	14	251	44	**295**	Apr.
Apr.			0	0	0	0	0	**0**	May
May			0	0	0	0	0	**0**	Jun.
Jun.	*L*	3	*237*	0	14	251	44	**295**	Jul.
Jul.			0	0	0	0	0	**0**	Aug.
Aug.			0	0	0	0	0	**0**	Sept.
Sept.			0	0	0	0	0	**0**	Oct.
Oct.			0	0	0	0	0	**0**	Nov.
Nov.			0	0	0	0	0	**0**	Dec.
Dec.			0	0	0	0	0	**0**	Jan.
			11,558	*7,360*	*1,135*	20,053	3,511	**£23,564**	

FIGURE E.2: *Fee management plan (continued)*

Note   The agreement with the client may require the architect to maintain records of services performed on a time basis, and of expenses and disbursements to be charged at net cost and to make these available to the client on reasonable request.

IVOR B'ARCH Architects LLP

RIBA ♯♯

Chartered Practice

Project: *Alterations at 16 Private Crescent*

Job no. *09/016*

Cumulative schedule of fees and expenses	Current work stage:	*EF*
	Application no.	*5*
	Up to and including:	*30 06 20X2*

Basic Fees		Basic Fee option	Basis	Works cost	% complete	£	
Stages	AB	Time	0%	0	100	0	*See Other Fees*
	CD	CLS	3.5%	100,000	100	3,500	
	EF	CLS	3.5%	94,800	50	1,659	
	GH	CLS	0.5%	0	0	0	*Transcription error*
	JK	CLS	4.0%	0	0	0	
	L	CLS	0.5%	0	0	0	
						5,159	

Other Fees	Hours	£		
Stage AB	8	662	100%	*This example based on calculated lump sums and expenses 6% of gross fee*
Survey	14	705	100%	
QS appointment	2	176	100%	
Visits to showrooms	14	1,150		
Interior design	15	1,100	50%	
See separate schedule for details		3,793	3,793	
Total fees			8,952	

Expenses					
Option 1	As paid		plus	0%	0	*See separate schedule*
Option 2		As % of gross fee		6%	537	
Other					0	537

Disbursements	*Planning fee*	800	
		0	800

Entries carried to fee account

FIGURE E.3: *Cumulative schedule of fees and expenses*

IVOR B'ARCH Architects LLP
Prospect Drive   Thawbridge BS17 2ZX
T: 0100 012012   **F:** 0100 012013   **E:** ivor@b'arch.com

VAT Reg. no: 987 6543-21

Fee account	Application for payment	*Serial no.:*	1001

This is not a tax invoice. A VAT invoice will be issued on receipt of payment.

To client	*Mr and Mrs Homeowner*	Application no.	*5*
Address	*16 Private Crescent*	Application date	*30 06 X2*
	Thawbridge BS17 5GH	Payment received	
Project:	*Alterations at 16 Private Crescent*	VAT invoice date	
Job no.	*09/016*	Tax point	

To professional services

Fees and other amounts due up to and including   *14 06 X2*

as the attached schedules and the agreement dated   *27 03 X2*

		£	VAT %	VAT £
	Fees	£8,952.00	*17.5%*	£1,566.60
	Expenses	£537.12	*17.5%*	£94.00
	Disbursements	£800.00	*0%*	£0.00
	Total due to date	£10,289.12		£1,660.60
Less:	Application no. *4*	£7,252.40		£1,129.17
	Balance due	£3,036.72		£531.43
	VAT now due	£531.43		
	Amount now claimed	**£3,568.15**		

Statement of account

To:	Application no. *4*	
	Fees and expenses	£7,252.40
	VAT	£1,129.17
		£8,381.57
Less:	*Payments received	£8,381.57
	Balance outstanding	£ –

*Payments received after 1st of the month are not shown here
Fax transmission: Please ensure that your retained copy is printed on plain paper
e-mail transmission: Please advise if any part of this account appears to be
                     incomplete or is indecipherable

FIGURE E.4: *Fee account*

IVOR B'ARCH Architects LLP
Prospect Drive   Thawbridge BS17 2ZX
T: 0100 012012   **F:** 0100 012013 **E:** ivor@b'arch.com

VAT Reg. no: 987 6543-21

RIBA
Chartered Practice

Fee account	~~Credit note (CR)~~	Debit note (DB)	*Serial no.:*	*1032*

This is not a tax invoice. A VAT invoice will be issued on receipt of payment.

To client	*Mr and Mrs Homeowner*	Application no./dated	**5DB**	*28 07 X2*
Address	*16 Private Crescent*	Application no./dated	*5*	*30 06 X2*
	Thawbridge BS17 5GH	Payment received	*5*	*27 07 X2*
Project:	*Alteration at 16 Private Crescent*	VAT invoice date	*5*	*27 07 X2*
Job no.	*09/016*	Tax point	*5*	*27 07 X2*

Reason:	*Correction of transcription error in schedule of fees and*				
	Application no. 5 dated 30 06 05	Correction			
	See revised schedule attached	£	VAT %	VAT £	
	Application no. **5DB**	£9,016.75	17.5%	£1,577.93	
	Expenses	£537.12	17.5%	£94.00	
	Disbursements	£800.00	0%	£0.00	
	Total due to date	£10,353.87		£1,671.93	
Less:	Application no. **5**	£10,289.12		£1,660.60	
	Balance due	£64.75		£11.33	
	VAT now due	£11.33			
	Amount now claimed	**£76.08**	To be added to next account		

Statement of account

To:	Application no. **5**			
	Fees and expenses	£10,289.12		
	VAT	£1,660.60		
		£11,949.72		
Less:	*Payments received	£11,949.72		
	Balance outstanding	£ –		

*Payments received after 1st of the month are not shown here

Fax transmission: Please ensure that your retained copy is printed on plain paper
e-mail transmission: Please advise if any part of this account appears to be
                            incomplete or is indecipherable

FIGURE E.5: *Credit/debit note*

Fee accounts, VAT and tax invoices

The following notes are based on applications for periodic payments first and issue of the tax invoice when payment is received. However, where a single payment for a service, perhaps a survey or a report, is due on completion, the tax invoice is issued immediately and is also the application for payment. The VAT requirements for invoices are not affected by the arrangement for VAT accounting by the architect (see below).

As noted in Section 7 (page 62), the agreement with the client should determine when applications for payment may be submitted and the method of calculating the amounts due. When a payment or part payment is due:

- four copies of the account are completed. Copy 1 should be titled 'Fee account – application for payment. This is not a tax invoice. A VAT invoice will be issued on receipt of payment'. Copies 2, 3 and 4 should be titled 'Fee account and tax invoice' and 'Client copy', 'File copy' and 'VAT file copy'
- the 'Application for payment' is sent to the client with a covering letter and any supporting calculations or schedules
- the other copies are retained with the job fee records or in a pending file until payment is received.

The transaction is not recorded in the practice's VAT accounts at this point.

When payment is received:

- on the date when payment is received, the invoice date and tax point are added to the retained copies
- one copy is sent to the client
- one copy is filed with the job fee records and one copy with the practice's VAT records.

The transaction should now be recorded in the practice's VAT accounts.

If a correction or change to the application is agreed before payment is received or before a tax invoice is issued:

- the original account and copies are cancelled but retained for reference
- a revised account marked 'Application no. X – Revised' is prepared and sent to the client.

If a tax invoice has been issued and a correction is necessary, for example for an error in calculation or transcription from schedule to account, a credit or debit note is issued to the client and 'File' and 'VAT file' copies are retained. The example in Figure E.5 demonstrates the format, but it is unlikely to be necessary for the amounts shown and the correction could be made in the next application.

VAT invoices

An architect who is registered for VAT is required to charge the tax and issue VAT invoices to the client except where the client is not registered for VAT. If using a standard proforma, these references can be deleted and/or marked 'not applicable'. If the architect is not registered for VAT at the time of completing the agreement it would be advisable to inform the client that, if the situation changes, VAT would become chargeable.

Under a contract, such as a RIBA Form, providing for stage payments for design, advisory and supervisory services, the tax point will usually be the date when a VAT invoice is issued or a payment is received, whichever happens first. Where only a single payment is due, the tax point will be the date on which the service is completed or payment is received or a tax invoice is issued, whichever is the earliest.

A tax invoice must include:

- an identifying number
- the tax point (date)
- the architect's name, address and VAT registration number
- the client's name and address
- the total amount payable (e.g. fees and expenses claimed) excluding tax
- the rate of tax, and
- the amount of tax charged.

More information can be found in HM Customs and Excise publications *The VAT Guide* (VAT Notice 700, April 2002; paragraph 15.3) and VAT Notice 708 *Buildings and Construction*.

VAT is payable by the client on the total bill for chargeable expenses, including any VAT paid by the architect. Note that, although some expenses may be zero rated, for instance a train ticket, the charge to the client will be standard rated, because the client is paying for the architect's services, not for buying a train ticket.

However, disbursements – that is amounts paid to third parties as agents of the client – should be shown separately in the invoice and be excluded when calculating the amount of VAT due on the architect's supply to the client.

It should be noted that, if a tax invoice is issued within 14 days after the date on which the services are completed, the tax point is the date when the invoice is issued. If the 14-day period is insufficient, application for an extension can be made to the local VAT office.

If VAT invoices are to be transmitted directly to a client's computer, the local VAT office, which must be given at least one month's notice of the intention, will explain the special conditions that apply. If VAT invoices are to be transmitted by e-mail, it is advisable that a note on the invoice requests clients to advise if the invoice is incomplete or indecipherable.

Tax invoices, once issued, cannot be altered. However, it is not necessary to adjust the original VAT charge, provided that both architect and client agree not to do so. Any correction to the tax liability must be done by means of either a credit note for overcharges or a debit note for undercharges.

The VAT element must be shown separately on both of these documents. Credit and debit notes must also be numbered serially and record copies kept. Spoilt and cancelled invoices must be kept for possible inspection by Customs and Excise. (See *The VAT Guide,* Notice 700, section 18.)

VAT accounting

The following methods of accounting for and payment of any VAT liability to HM Customs and Excise may be suitable for architectural practices.

Cash accounting (see VAT Notice 731, July 2008)

Under the cash accounting scheme, if turnover is less than £1.6 million (£150,000 for the flat rate scheme) VAT is accounted for on the basis of payments received. This could be particularly beneficial:

- if the client insists that the application for payment is also the tax invoice
- if the client is a late payer
- in the event of non-payment, as the VAT is not payable.

Annual accounting (see VAT Notice 732, April 2006)

Under the annual accounting scheme, if turnover is less than £1.35 million, this scheme provides for submission of one VAT return each year. Interim instalments, usually $9 \times 10\%$ of the anticipated liability, are required with a balancing payment and the VAT return must be made within two months of the year end.

Flat rate scheme (FRS) for small businesses (see VAT Notice 733, March 2007)

Where turnover is less than £150,000, under this flat rate scheme it is not necessary to identify and record the VAT on sales and purchases to calculate the VAT liability. It is only necessary to record business sales and apply a flat rate percentage to the total in each period to calculate the VAT liability.

The flat rate scheme may be used in conjunction with the annual accounting scheme but has its own version of cash accounting. The flat rate percentage for architects is 12.5% (March 2007).

Bibliography and useful websites

Bibliography

Good Practice Guide Series, RIBA Publishing

Keeping Out of Trouble, Owen Luder, 3rd edition (2006)
Painless Financial Management, Brian Pinder-Ayres (2008)
Starting a Practice, Simon Foxell (2006)

Other publications

Architects' Guide to Fee Bidding, M. Paul Nicholson, Spon Press (2002)
The Architect's Guide to Running a Practice, David Littlefield, Architectural Press (2005)
Architect's Handbook of Practice Management (*The Handbook*), Sarah Lupton, RIBA Publications, 7th edition (2001), in particular Section 13, *Claiming Fees*
Getting Paid, Nicholas J. Carnell and Steven Yakeley, RIBA Publications (2003)
A Guide to Managing IT, Richard Watson and Steven Lockley, RIBA Publications (2001)
The Late Payment of Commercial Debts (Interest) Act 1998: A user's guide, The Better Payment Practice Group
Spon's Architects and Builders Price Book – Part 1 Fees for professional services, Taylor and Francis (2007)
The Value of Architecture: Context and Current Thinking, Eric Loe, RIBA Future Studies (2000)

Websites referred to in this guide

BCIS	www.bcis.co.uk
Business needs	www.bre.co.uk/clip
	www.businesslink.gov.uk
	www.shellstep.org.uk
	www.constructionline.co.uk
	www.fsb.org.uk (Federation of Small Businesses)
Fees	www.feesbureau.co.uk
	www.colander.co.uk
Time and cost systems	www.archioffice.com
	www.framework-software.com
	www.paprika-software.com
KPIs	www.constructingexcellence.org.uk
Payment	www.paymentscorer.com
	www.payontime.co.uk
	www.creditmanagement.org.uk/berrguides.htm
Debt collection	www.insolvency.gov.uk/pdfs/forms/6-1.pdf
	www.moneyclaim.gov.uk
Acts of parliament	www.opsi.gov.uk/
Statutory regulations	www.opsi.gov.uk/stat

Index

Note: page numbers in italics refer to figures and tables